From the contributors to our pastor-teacher,

John MacArthur.

*Thank you, John, for faithfully showing us,
both through your preaching and your life,
what it means to be a man of the Word.*

*We are blessed beyond measure to
have served at Grace Community Church
under your leadership.*

Contents

Foreword:

Real Men Walk with God

JOHN MACARTHUR

E xamine the lives of the righteous men in Scripture and one
common characteristic quickly surfaces—they all walked
with God, in sweet communion with Him and sincere commitment to Him. The patterns of their lives matched the passion
of their hearts: to know the Lord and obey Him. Like Enoch, they
walked with God in private devotion and intimate fellowship (Genesis 5:22-24). Like Noah, they walked with God in public displays of
righteousness, even when the culture around them was totally corrupt (Genesis 6:9). Like Abraham, they walked with Him in their
personal decisions, even when God called them to believe His seemingly impossible promises (Genesis 17:1). The priority of their lives
was to honor the Lord in everything, and they acted accordingly.

These faithful men called others to walk with God too. Moses
and Joshua, for example, repeatedly reminded the Israelites "to walk
in His ways" (Deuteronomy 8:6; cf. 10:12; Joshua 22:5). The Lord
promised His people that if they walked with Him, He would likewise walk with them. As He told them in Leviticus 26, "If you walk
in My statutes and keep My commandments so as to carry them
out...I will also walk among you and be your God, and you shall be
My people" (verses 3,12). What an amazing promise!

Yet only a few generations later, the people would turn and walk away from God (Judges 2:17,22). From the time of the Judges to the Babylonian captivity, seasons of national disobedience and divine chastisement plagued Israel. There were still some who walked with God—leaders like David (1 Kings 3:14), Hezekiah (2 Kings 20:3), and Josiah (2 Kings 22:2; 23:3). But many of the nation's rulers walked in paths of idolatry and immorality (see 2 Kings 8:18; 10:31; 16:3; 21:21). Though the prophets continually called them to "walk in the light of the Lord" (Isaiah 2:5; cf. Jeremiah 26:4; Ezekiel 20:19; Hosea 14:9; Micah 4:5), the people did not listen. And as a result, both the northern and southern kingdoms eventually fell to their enemies.

King David, in particular, had known the critical importance and unimaginable joy of walking with God. He charged his son Solomon to do the same (1 Kings 2:3)—and Solomon, at least at first, seemed eager to heed his father's instruction (1 Kings 8:58). It's no wonder, then, that the books of Psalms and Proverbs are filled with encouragement to walk in God's ways (for example, Psalms 81:13; 119:3; 128:1). Men who do so walk in integrity (Psalm 15:2), blamelessly (Psalm 101:6), and according to God's commands (Psalm 119:1,35). They do not follow the paths of the wicked (Psalm 1:1; Proverbs 4:14), but walk in uprightness (Proverbs 14:2) and wisdom (Proverbs 28:26). And as a result they receive God's blessing. As Solomon wrote, "The perverse in heart are an abomination to the LORD, but the blameless in their walk are His delight" (Proverbs 11:20).

When we come to the New Testament, walking with God is still a prominent theme. Believers must not walk according to the flesh (Romans 8:4) or their former way of life (Ephesians 4:17). Rather, they are to walk in the Spirit (Galatians 5:16,25), in newness of life (Romans 6:4), in love (Ephesians 5:2), in good works (Ephesians 2:10), in truth (2 John 4), and in a manner worthy of the Lord (Colossians 1:10; 1 Thessalonians 4:1). They are to walk by faith (2 Corinthians 5:7), as children of light (Ephesians 5:8; 1 John 1:7), as wise men (Ephesians 5:15), according to God's commandments (2 John 6), even as Christ Himself walked (1 John 2:6). As they run the race of faith, they must keep their eyes on Christ (Hebrews 12:2). And they can also find encouragement by looking back to the faithful examples of the Old Testament saints (Hebrews 11:1–12:1).

Like believers in Bible times, Christian men today are called to walk in obedience, truth, and godliness. Of course, nothing in our world makes this easy. The culture is only getting worse; and the church, in many cases, has become weak and shallow. Those who stand for purity of life and purity of doctrine are often derided as being out of touch or unloving. The temptation to compromise is great. But God is looking for those who will remain faithful. As 2 Chronicles 16:9 reminds us, "The eyes of the LORD move to and fro throughout the earth that He may strongly support those whose heart is completely His." The actions of godly men are not dictated by peer pressure or public opinion. Rather, they stem from deep personal character and conviction—the kind that is forged over years of walking with the Lord in intimate fellowship and submissive obedience.

That is why I am delighted to commend this book to you. It is a clarion call for Christian men to step up to the plate and embrace all that God intends for them. Unlike so many other books for men, which substitute human wisdom for biblical instruction, *Men of the Word* looks to the Scriptures to see what God says about being a man who honors Him. That, of course, is where any definition of true manhood must begin. If you are to be a real man, in the eyes of God, you must understand what it is He calls you to be. To do that, you must start with His Word, which is exactly what this book does. That is what makes it so invaluable—a must-read for any man who desires to grow in godliness.

But this book is special to me for another reason. Not only is its content superb and its message desperately needed, but its authors comprise a group of men whom I love and respect dearly—my co-workers in ministry, the pastoral staff of Grace Community Church. There is no group of men I could more heartily endorse than these men. They are truly men of the Word. It is a joy for me to see them produce this volume because I have seen them faithfully model these truths throughout our years of ministry together. I know you will be blessed by their efforts here.

In the pages that follow, you will be encouraged as you read about the saints of old—men like Abraham, Daniel, and Paul, who honored the Lord through their faithfulness to Him. You will be reminded of the standard to which God has called you, as one who desires to obey His Word. You will be challenged to stand firm, exhorted to live righteously, refreshed by God's truth, and comforted by His grace. Through it all, you will inevitably see a recurring theme. It has been the theme of this short foreword. It is the theme of every godly man's life. And it should be the theme of yours as well: *Real men walk with God.*

If that is your heart, turn the page and keep reading.

The Key to Becoming a Godly Man

From the outset, two points need to be made about this book. On one hand, *this is a book about real men.* It was written by pastors to Christian men to encourage them toward true masculinity—manhood as God defines it in His Word. It is not an exhaustive study, but one we hope will encourage you toward greater Christlikeness. As we look at the lives of various biblical characters, gleaning from the lessons they learned, we will quickly find that being a real man has nothing to do with one's physical strength, athletic ability, financial wealth, or social status. Rather, it has everything to do with personal integrity, heartfelt obedience, and daily dependence on the Lord. Humility, faith, and love are the traits that characterize a real man—the kind who finds favor with God.

On the other hand, *this book is not really about men at all.* Let me explain what I mean.

My earliest memories include the stories of great biblical heroes, usually presented as flannel-graph characters or picture-Bible portraits. There were Adam and Eve, Cain and Abel, Jacob and Esau, Joseph and his brothers, Moses and the Israelites, and a myriad of others. I loved listening to accounts of how Samson defeated a lion with his bare hands, Jonathan protected his best friend David, and Esther convinced her husband to spare the Jews. In every story, the point was always the same: God is faithful to those who walk with Him.

In this book, we will consider the lives of some of the most beloved biblical characters—men who walked with God in faithful obedience. We will be encouraged by their fortitude, warned by their failures, and uplifted by their unwavering faith. Yet it is important to emphasize that the focus is not really on them. Whatever their successes and triumphs, all the credit goes to God. Their stories of faith, however valiant, are not intended to exalt them. Rather, they are witnesses to God's incredible faithfulness. He is the One to whom they looked for help and deliverance—and He never failed them.

The epic accounts of biblical history are, most fundamentally, testimonies to God's mighty power. He is the main character in every story, from the parting of the Red Sea to the crumbling of Jericho's walls to the toppling of the giant Goliath. All of these accounts are Sunday school classics. They feature men like Moses, Joshua, and David. But ultimately, and more importantly, they magnify the greatness and glory of God.

This is not to say that we can't learn valuable lessons from the godly men of biblical history. Certainly we can (and we will in this book). Their lives were recorded to serve "as an example" and "for our instruction" (1 Corinthians 10:11). As "so great a cloud of witnesses" (Hebrews 12:1), they leave behind a legacy of faithfulness that we are called to follow. Yet their successes and triumphs were not the result of their own cleverness or strength. Only as they depended on God, trusting fully in His wisdom and power, were they able to accomplish anything of lasting value. And that is a critically important lesson for us to remember. Though we can benefit greatly from their examples, we must always keep our eyes on Christ as we press toward the heavenly prize (Hebrews 12:2). Staying focused on Him is the key to becoming a godly man.

With that in mind, may the Lord be honored through your study of this book.

Real Men Live by Faith
Lessons from the Life of Abraham

Nathan Busenitz

I t has become popular in our society to talk about *faith* as though it were some sort of mystical force or magical power. Countless movies, television shows, and songs reinforce the idea that you can achieve any goal and overcome any challenge *if only you have a little faith* or *if only you just believe.* Whether that faith is placed "in yourself" or in some other fantastical force (like the power of love or the promise of change), the point is always the same: Believe hard enough, and dreams can come true. To our postmodern culture, *what* people believe in is not all that important. The critical thing is simply that they *believe*, and that their faith—whatever its object—makes them happy and furthers their lifestyle.

Biblical faith could not be more opposite. It is defined by a confident trust in and full dependence on the only right object of faith—God Himself. The reality is that faith is only as good as the object on which it rests. For the postmodern secularist, having faith "in yourself" is an extremely limiting and discouraging prospect. Faith based on that kind of fantasy is nothing more than fiction. But for the Christian, faith in God is the key to facing any circumstance of life. God is infinitely powerful, wise, good, faithful, and loving. To depend on Him is to say with the apostle Paul, "If God is for us, who is against us?...For I am convinced that neither death, nor life, nor angels, nor principalities, nor things present, nor things to come, nor powers, nor height, nor depth, nor any other created thing, will be able to separate us from the love of God, which is in Christ Jesus our Lord" (Romans 8:31,38-39).

When we read about the heroes of the faith in Hebrews 11, we learn that "by faith [they] conquered kingdoms, performed acts of righteousness, obtained promises, shut the mouths of lions, quenched the power of fire, escaped the edge of the sword, from weakness were made strong, became mighty in war, put foreign armies to flight. Women [even] received back their dead [sons] by resurrection" (verses 33-35). Through faith, the Old Testament saints accomplished some incredible things. Or perhaps better stated, *God* accomplished incredible things through those who believed in Him. That is an important clarification. The biblical heroes did not simply believe; they believed *in God.* Their faith was unseen, but it was not blind. God was the source of their power and strength. He was their focus and the object of their faith. Their confident trust and full dependence was placed in Him.

Void of the right object, faith is nothing more than wishful thinking. It is pitiful and powerless. But placed in God, faith is the essence of salvation and the heart of the Christian life. The pages of Scripture are filled with examples of people who walked by faith. One of the foremost was a man from Mesopotamia who, while childless, left his homeland to follow God, and as a result became the father of a great nation.

A MAN NAMED ABRAHAM

Abraham is one of the most famous and beloved characters from all of biblical history. His story, found in Genesis 11–25, has been retold countless times—from the rabbis of Old Testament Israel to the Sunday school teachers of today. He has been the subject of songs, sermons, books, and theological discussions. Both the Jews and the Arabs look to him as their physical ancestor; and the New Testament declares him to be the spiritual father of all who believe (Romans 4:11-12; Galatians 3:29). The Lord certainly kept His promise to Abraham when He told him, "[I will] make your name great" (Genesis 12:2).

It is easy for us, over 4000 years later, to take Abraham's life for granted. We've heard the stories so many times that we already know how everything will turn out. Yet unlike us, Abraham did not have the luxury of knowing exactly how the story would end. He simply had to trust God for the future, living by faith in the midst of daily trials and temptations.

As with all of us, there were times when Abraham did not trust the Lord as he should have (see Genesis 20, for example). Yet on the whole, his life was characterized by a steadfast faith in God and His Word. Even when the fulfillment of God's promises to Abraham went far beyond his own lifetime, he continued to trust and obey. It's no wonder that the New Testament looks back to his life as a model of faith that all believers should follow.

In this chapter, we will consider four lessons that Abraham's example teaches us about being men of faith.

1. *Men of Faith Submit to God's Plan*

The year was 2091 BC, and Abraham (who was then called *Abram*) was 75 years old. Though born in Ur, his family had since moved to a town named Haran, located in northeastern Mesopotamia (modern-day Iraq), just east of the Euphrates River.

Abraham was a first-generation believer. According to Joshua 24:2, he had grown up in a pagan family. Being from Ur, he had probably been raised as a worshiper of the Sumerian moon god Nannar, also called Sin. Abraham's father, Terah, may have even been named after this deity, since his name is derived from the Hebrew word for moon.[1]

The Jewish historian Josephus recorded that Abraham was, in fact, a great astronomer.[2] When the Lord saved him, Abraham realized that the sun, moon, and stars were not gods, but only created bodies operating according to God's grand design. The astonished stargazer, armed with a new understanding of the universe, soon began to publicly denounce the astrology of his neighbors. But they did not want to listen. His faithful proclamations about the true God were met with what Josephus called a "tumult" of opposition.

It is in that context that God told Abraham to move his family to Canaan, promising to make a great nation of his descendants (Genesis 12:1-3). What a promise! Yet for Abraham it meant leaving behind everything he had ever known—including the home where he had settled and the place his father died. The call to leave tested whether he truly believed the Lord. Almost surely it would have been easier to stay in Haran, where things were familiar to him. He had never been to Canaan, the land to which God commanded him to go.

But Abraham didn't make excuses or complain (see Genesis 12:4-5). Instead, he responded in obedient faith, as the author of Hebrews explained: "By faith Abraham, when he was called, obeyed by going out to a place which he was to receive for an inheritance; and he went out, not knowing where he was going" (Hebrews 11:8). Though his path was unknown to him, Abraham submitted to God's plan, confident that the Lord would send him exactly where he needed to be. His own preference might have been to stay in Haran. But he obeyed the Lord's command without hesitation, knowing that God's will was best even if it required a dramatic life change.

2. Men of Faith Rest in God's Justice

Upon settling in the land of Canaan, Abraham and his nephew

Lot decided to part ways because their herds of livestock were getting too large to keep together. Abraham graciously gave his nephew first choice as to where he would raise his flocks. So Lot selected the most fertile land for himself, near the cities of Sodom and Gomorrah.

In this case, the greener grass was not the better choice. The cities that bordered Lot's pastures were incredibly wicked. And Lot soon came under their influence. He eventually settled in Sodom (Genesis 13:12-13)—a place so perverse that its name is a synonym for debauchery. Sodom's sin was so hateful to God that He determined to destroy it with fire from heaven.

When Abraham learned of the Lord's intention, he interceded for the city—not in defense of its wickedness but so that God might spare any righteous people who lived there (Genesis 18:20-33). It was, after all, the home of Lot and his family. Abraham likely knew others in the city too because, some time earlier, he had rescued Sodom's inhabitants from an invading army (Genesis 14:1-16). After Abraham pleaded on the city's behalf, God assured him that even if there were only ten righteous people there, He would not destroy it (Genesis 18:32).

But there were not even ten righteous souls in Sodom. According to Genesis 19, there was only one righteous man (cf. 2 Peter 2:7) and he was far from perfect. Though Lot was rescued, along with his two daughters, Sodom was utterly destroyed. Yet Abraham's intercession proved that he knew God to be a patient executioner—One who wielded His anger carefully and only with just cause.

Abraham's confidence in God's perfect justice is especially evident in Genesis 18:25, where he said to the Lord, "Far be it from You to do such a thing, to slay the righteous with the wicked, so that the righteous and the wicked are treated alike. Far be it from You! Shall not the Judge of all the earth deal justly?" The Lord's perfect character, as Abraham knew, meant that even in dispensing His wrath the right thing would be done. Though Sodom would be destroyed, Abraham had no reason to doubt God's righteous goodness.

In our own day, many people wrestle with the implications of divine wrath. The question is often asked, "If God is love, how can He punish sinners both in this life and the next?" The answer, as Abraham's example illustrates, is ultimately found in God's righteous character. His wisdom is faultless and His judgments are pure. Knowing that God is gracious, Abraham fervently interceded for the city of Sodom. Then, knowing that God is holy and just, he rested confidently in the fact that the Judge of all the earth will always do what is right.

3. Men of Faith Wait on God's Timing

In Genesis 17, God promised Abraham that he would have a son through his wife Sarah. But there was a problem. Both Abraham and Sarah were very old, and Sarah had been barren her whole life. Nevertheless, God's promise was clear: "I will bless her [Sarah], and indeed I will give you a son by her. Then I will bless her, and she shall be a mother of nations; kings of peoples will come from her" (Genesis 17:16). In fact, when the Lord visited Abraham in chapter 18, He reiterated this guarantee: "I will surely return to you at this time next year; and behold, Sarah your wife will have a son" (verse 10).

Sarah's response, when she heard what God said, was probably the same reaction we would have had if we had been in her situation. She laughed in disbelief, wondering how she and Abraham could possibly bear a child at their advanced age (Genesis 18:11-12). Abraham too had initially responded with doubt-filled laughter (see Genesis 17:17). Yet Romans 4:19-21 indicates that his disposition soon changed to one of confident hope: "Without becoming weak in faith he contemplated his own body, now as good as dead since he was about a hundred years old, and the deadness of Sarah's womb; yet, with respect to the promise of God, he did not waver in unbelief but grew strong in faith, giving glory to God, and being fully assured that what God had promised, He was able also to perform." Even when childbearing seemed physically impossible,

Abraham chose to believe God's promises rather than focus on the scientific impossibilities of his situation. And God was faithful (see Genesis 21:1-2).

Through their newborn son, God would fulfill His promise to make of Abraham a great nation, as numerous as the stars in the sky (Genesis 15:5). That promise must have been particularly meaningful to Abraham, given his background in astronomy. He and Sarah, in their old age, finally had the baby boy they had awaited for so long. Their son's name, Isaac (meaning "laughter"), pointed both to their initial disbelief in God's promise and the subsequent joy they found in His faithfulness. God had assured Abraham, years before, "'I WILL SURELY BLESS YOU AND I WILL SURELY MULTIPLY YOU.' And so, having patiently waited, he obtained the promise" (Hebrews 6:14-15).

In waiting on the Lord for Isaac's birth, Abraham learned to trust God in everything. That lesson was vitally important because it helped prepare the aged patriarch for an even greater test—when God would ask him to give up the very son he loved.

4. Men of Faith Hope in God's Provision

In Genesis 22, God tested Abraham's faith to see exactly where his hope had truly been placed. The Lord said to Abraham, "Take now your son, your only son, whom you love, Isaac, and go to the region of Moriah, and offer him there as a burnt offering on one of the mountains of which I will tell you" (verse 2).

It is difficult to imagine what Abraham might have thought when he heard those words—maybe something like: *What is going on? This is the son whom You gave us, Lord, in our old age. When we thought there was no hope of having children, You gave us this boy. Your promise to me about being the father of a great nation is based on this child. He is the descendant who makes it all possible. And now You want me to sacrifice him? There must be some mistake.*

Yet if Abraham had any doubts, they didn't last long. God had already proven His faithfulness to Abraham in the birth of Isaac. So when Abraham was asked to do the seemingly unthinkable, he responded with confident trust and without complaint.

As Abraham and Isaac approached the place for the sacrifice, Isaac noticed that something was missing. He asked his father, "Behold, the fire and wood [are here], but where is the lamb for the burnt offering?" Abraham's faith-filled reply was anchored in his right theology: "God will provide for Himself the lamb for the burnt offering, my son" (Genesis 22:7-8). Just moments later, when they reached the designated spot, Abraham tied up his son and prepared to slay him. What could he have been thinking at that moment? According to Hebrews 11:19, as he lifted the knife, Abraham "considered that God was able even to raise [Isaac] from the dead" (ESV). He was so confident in God's promises that he reasoned, even if his son were to be killed, God would bring him back from the dead. Talk about faith! God had promised to raise up a great nation through Isaac (Genesis 15:5-21), and Abraham knew He would keep His word.

In Genesis 22:12-14, we read that God stopped Abraham from killing his son, instead providing for the sacrifice a ram caught in a nearby thicket. That provision not only spared Isaac's life, it also pictured the once-for-all provision of Christ on the cross—whereby sinners are saved through His substitutionary sacrifice. Appropriately, "Abraham called the name of that place The LORD Will Provide, as it is said to this day, 'In the mount of the LORD it will be provided'" (verse 14).

Abraham had demonstrated that he was willing to trust the Lord with everything that he had, including his own son. His confidence in God's promises never wavered; he knew the Lord would provide. Through his actions, he proved that his life was governed by both a God-centered focus and a God-grounded faith.

SAVED BY GRACE THROUGH FAITH

Our study of Abraham would be incomplete if we did not

consider one crucial aspect of his life. In Romans 4, the apostle Paul used Abraham's example to explain the heart of the gospel—namely, that salvation is by grace through faith in Christ alone and not on the basis of works. Like every believer before or since, Abraham was justified by faith. Commenting on Genesis 15:6, Paul wrote, "For what does the Scripture say? 'ABRAHAM BELIEVED GOD, AND IT WAS CREDITED TO HIM AS RIGHTEOUSNESS.' Now to the one who works, his wage is not credited as a favor, but as what is due. But to the one who does not work, but believes in Him who justifies the ungodly, his faith is credited as righteousness" (Romans 4:3-5). The apostle's point was that Abraham was saved not on the basis of his own self-righteous deeds, but through faith. His right standing before God was a gift of divine grace, credited to him through no effort or merit of his own. He did nothing to earn his salvation. He simply believed God, and even his faith was a gift of grace, as it is for every believer (Ephesians 2:8).

By faith, Abraham trusted fully in God for his salvation. The same must be true for anyone who desires forgiveness from God and fellowship with Him. In faith, the sinner must recognize his spiritual bankruptcy, crying out for mercy and clinging to the cross. Only those who have been covered with the righteousness of Christ—their sins paid for through His sacrificial death—can enjoy a right standing before God. To quote again from Paul, "Now not for [Abraham's] sake only was it written that it was credited to him [as righteousness], but for our sake also, to whom it will be credited, as those who believe in Him who raised Jesus our Lord from the dead, He who was delivered over because of our transgressions, and was raised because of our justification" (Romans 4:23-25). Later in Romans, the apostle reiterated the gospel message with these words: "If you confess with your mouth Jesus as Lord, and believe in your heart that God raised him from the dead, you will be saved" (10:9).

At the outset of a book on godly manhood, it is crucial to emphasize that real masculinity—the kind that pleases God—is impossible apart from saving faith in Christ. The life of faith begins at the moment of regeneration. And those who have not yet experienced God's transforming grace cannot know the sweetness of growing in Christlikeness or walking in His Spirit. Like Abraham, we are called to walk in faith. And like Abraham, that faith begins at the moment of salvation.

LIVING BY FAITH LIKE ABRAHAM DID

Time and again throughout his life, Abraham responded with confident trust in God—even when, from his perspective, the future seemed uncertain. When he could have stayed in Haran, he submitted to God's plan instead. When Sodom was about to be destroyed, he rested in God's righteous character and perfect justice. When he was too old to have children, he believed God's promise. Even when the Lord's command seemed unreasonable—asking Abraham to sacrifice his precious son Isaac—he still placed his hope in God's provision.

In each of these decisions, Abraham put his full confidence in the Lord. Though he did not always know what the outcome would be, he had no reason to doubt or grow anxious. God had everything under control, and Abraham was content to rest in Him, knowing He is faithful. That is the essence of faith—full dependence on our sovereign God both for this life and the life to come.

When we place our hope in the Lord and follow His Word, we demonstrate the same kind of faith that characterized Abraham. To *trust and obey* is not just a well-known lyric; it is the heartbeat of a godly life. Though Abraham was not perfect, his life was marked by that kind of steadfast confidence in God. As such, he serves as a fitting example for us to emulate.

2

Real Men Find Satisfaction in God
Lessons from the Life of Solomon

RICK HOLLAND

F ew would ascribe scholarly credentials to rock-and-roll icon Mick Jagger. Yet few have more succinctly described humanity's plight. Jagger canonized man's exasperated quest in the lyrics of a hit song in 1965. The familiar chorus bemoans the inability to get any satisfaction in life. Jagger is no sage, but his confession is no less true.

Mick Jagger was not the first to attach a catchphrase to man's frustration with life. The tenth-century BC version of an inability to get satisfaction is "Vanity of vanities! All is vanity" (Ecclesiastes 1:2). Satisfaction remains an elusive aspiration, just as it has been since the writing of Ecclesiastes some thirty centuries ago.

THE PURSUIT OF SATISFACTION

The life of Solomon exemplifies the cul-de-sac of mankind's undeniable search for satisfaction. Solomon learned the hard way that, outside of God, the pursuit of happiness leads only from one dead end to another. As a son of King David, he had fame and a noble heritage; as a man of God-given wisdom, he had unequalled intellectual capabilities; as the king of Israel, he had absolute power and authority; and as the richest monarch in Israel's history, he had access to inexhaustible wealth. In other words, he had the popularity, the brains, the means, and the money to do whatever he wanted to do—and he put it all toward the pursuit of his own happiness.

But at the end of it all, Solomon discovered it was nothing more than a façade. His reflections and conclusions, based on the pain and disappointment of his own personal experiences, are recorded for us in the book of Ecclesiastes. They serve as a needed reminder for you, me, and anyone else who might be tempted to think that happiness can be bought, or that the grass is greener on the other side of the proverbial fence. Take it from one of the richest, smartest, and most powerful men who ever lived: You can't find satisfaction anywhere other than God.

After years of living the "good life," Solomon looked back on it all and called it vanity. He described his exploits as a breath or vapor—like the steam that rises from a cup of coffee and disappears into thin air. What seemed like fun in the moment turned out to have no lasting value. It was worthless, transient, and fleeting. Like a shiny gumball, the pleasures of this world tasted great initially, but they soon lost their flavor. The treasure box of temporal pursuits had looked so glamorous from the outside; but now, having opened it, Solomon found it empty.

THE FOLLY OF A WISE MAN

When God first spoke to Solomon, He gave the young king an unprecedented opportunity. Appearing to him in a dream, God said, "Ask what you wish Me to give you" (1 Kings 3:5). Solomon responded with a humble request: "Give Your servant an understanding heart to judge Your people to discern between good and evil. For who is able to judge this great people of Yours?" (verse 9).

God was pleased to give Solomon the wisdom he sought. So much so, in fact, that He promised to grant him riches and honor as well.

Yet in spite of the heavenly wisdom he had received, Solomon would make some very foolish choices. This is most clearly seen in whom he chose to marry. Not only did Solomon have many wives (which was a major problem in itself!), he was utterly careless when it came to discerning a potential mate's spiritual character. As a result, he found himself surrounded by a harem of godless women, and the consequences were disastrous. "For when Solomon was old, his wives turned his heart away after other gods; and his heart was not wholly devoted to the LORD his God" (1 Kings 11:4). Sadly, having shifted his affections away from God, Solomon sought satisfaction in other places. But in the end, he learned that true joy, meaning, and fulfillment can't be found anywhere else.

SOLOMON'S EXPERIMENT WITH PLEASURE

In Ecclesiastes 2, Solomon outlined his failed attempts to find happiness and satisfaction in the things of this world. He wrote in verse 1, "I said to myself, 'Come now, I will test you with pleasure. So enjoy yourself.'" Thinking that temporal pleasures could offer lasting joy, Solomon set off to find happiness through any means possible. He denied himself no luxury and pursued his every desire (2:10). His unrestricted power (1 Kings 4:21), unlimited resources (1 Kings 10:14-20), and unrivaled wisdom (1 Kings 3:12) made it possible for him to do whatever he wanted. If anyone were ever in a position to find true happiness in the things of this life, it was Solomon. But whatever role he played in his quest for meaning and fulfillment— whether as a philosopher (1:12-15), student (1:16-18), party animal (2:1-2), alcoholic (2:3), workaholic (2:4-8a), entertainer (2:8b), playboy (2:8c), competitor (2:9-11), intellectual (2:12-16), or philanthropist (2:17-23)—he repeatedly came up empty-handed.

Solomon searched for satisfaction in at least seven areas: fun, alcohol, materialism, entertainment, romance, accomplishment, and wisdom. Not much has changed since Solomon's time. Our society looks to those same pleasures and pursuits, trying desperately to find lasting happiness in them. But what a lesson we can learn from Solomon's experience! Rather than repeating his failed experiments, we can benefit from his conclusions. Solomon's wasted life serves as a needed warning to us: Don't spend your time, money, and energy chasing the empty idols of this earth. "The world is passing away, and also its lusts," the apostle John wrote in 1 John 2:17. It is *not* the right place to find true meaning and joy.

Looking for Life at the Party (Ecclesiastes 2:2)

Solomon began his quest for happiness the same place that many do today: in having fun. He looked for satisfaction in *laughter* and *pleasure*—two words that describe the amusing delight of games and parties. Celebrating, socializing, joking and laughing, enjoying oneself: Were these the keys to ultimate happiness?

If anyone could throw a good party, it surely would have been Solomon. First Kings 4:22-23 describes the enormous amounts of food needed for his daily feasts. These were much more than just backyard barbeques! His popularity as the king meant that every member of Israel's high society wanted to attend. His wealth made it possible to host celebrations that were unsurpassed in extravagance. Even his wisdom, applied creatively to each occasion, would have made every social event uniquely spectacular and entertaining. Solomon's galas were the talk of the entire nation. And he was the life of the party (cf. 1 Kings 10:24).

But what did Solomon himself say about the festivities? The laughter of the party is "madness" (Ecclesiastes 2:2). Proverbs 14:13 records the same verdict—laughter is unable to sustain joy and happiness. At the end of all his fun, Solomon was left with one haunting question—"What does it accomplish?" (Ecclesiastes 2:2).

The king certainly enjoyed the high life a party could offer. But in the end, he realized that it could not provide enduring happiness. This is not to say that we can't enjoy fellowship and fun in the context of wholesome Christian community. Of course we can! But we must be careful to remember Solomon's point: *Fun and games* can't bring true fulfillment and joy to your life. As the wisest man came to understand, eventually the party will come to an end. So if you are searching for a happiness that lasts, you will have to find it somewhere else.

Looking for Life in a Buzz (Ecclesiastes 2:3)

When his social life didn't satisfy him, Solomon turned to his next pursuit: alcohol. Maybe he could find happiness at the bottom of a wine glass. As he wrote in verse 3, "I explored with my mind how to stimulate my body with wine." Yet his mental powers were such that, even when he was drunk, his "mind was guiding [him] wisely."

If anyone had access to the most exotic and powerful alcoholic beverages of that day, it was Solomon. He knew enough about it to write in Proverbs 20:1, "Wine is a mocker, strong drink a brawler, and whoever is intoxicated by it is not wise." A lengthy section at the end of Proverbs 23 echoes these same sentiments:

> Who has woe? Who has sorrow? Who has contentions? Who has complaining? Who has wounds without cause? Who has redness of eyes? Those who linger long over wine, those who go to taste mixed wine. Do not look on the wine when it is red, when it sparkles in the cup, when it goes down smoothly; at the last it bites like a serpent and stings like a viper. Your eyes will see strange things and your mind will utter perverse things. And you will be like one who lies down in the middle of the sea, or like one who lies down on the top of a mast. [The drunkard says,] "They struck me, but I did not become ill; they beat me, but I did not know it. When shall I awake? I will seek another drink" (verses 29-35).

Yet Solomon, neglectful of his own wisdom, poured himself into a life of intoxication and drunkenness. And, like any number of country music singers, he found his life to be as empty as the last bottle he had finished.

As Solomon explained, the goal of his experiment was to "see what good there is for the sons of men to do under heaven the few years of their lives" (Ecclesiastes 2:3). Like many today, Solomon thought that life might make more sense if his senses were under the influence. But as he soon learned, the "buzz" always wears off right before the headache and nausea start. Drinking might seem to temporarily mask life's pain, but it certainly couldn't bring him the happiness he sought. Solomon's discovery was sobering: True meaning and lasting fulfillment can't be found in alcohol.

Looking for Life in Material Possessions (Ecclesiastes 2:4-8a)

The next pleasure Solomon tested was materialism. Not wanting to leave anything out, he devoted more space to describing this pleasure than the previous two. In so doing, he revealed the real focus of his heart with the oft-repeated phrase "for myself." It occurs six times in verses 4-8, evidencing the self-centeredness of his efforts.

In surveying his substantial acquisitions, Solomon began with his many building projects, including various works, houses, vineyards, gardens, parks, and man-made lakes and forests. He continued by noting his many servants, flocks, and herds, along with his vast collection of silver and gold, and "the treasure of kings and provinces" (verse 8). By ancient standards, Solomon was filthy rich. In fact, according to 2 Chronicles 9:22, he was the richest man in the world. If *Forbes* magazine had been keeping a list back then of the world's richest people, Solomon would have been at the top. And because he had the financial resources to purchase anything he wanted, Solomon quickly mastered the business of obtaining.

Imagine what your life might be like if you had inexhaustible riches. Perhaps you would collect fancy cars, invest in luxurious houses, dress in expensive suits, and travel the globe in your own private jet. But could these possessions bring you true happiness? Our culture certainly seems to think so. Hence, the booming credit card business. But what did Solomon find? He had more money and more stuff than you and I will ever have. Yet in the end he found that it was "all vanity and striving after wind" (verse 11). Later in Ecclesiastes he would say it even more directly: "He who loves money will not be satisfied with money, nor he who loves abundance with its income. This too is vanity" (5:10). After the shopping spree of a lifetime, with no spending limit of any kind, Solomon's conclusion was this: True satisfaction can't be found in the things you build or buy. As our Lord said in Luke 12:15, "Not even when one has an abundance does his life consist of his possessions."

Looking for Life in Entertainment (Ecclesiastes 2:8b)

When Solomon found materialism to be empty, he moved on to entertainment. He wrote, "I provided for myself male and female singers" (2:8). Like so many before and since, the king thought he could find true meaning through the leading form of entertainment in his day—music. Of course, music is still one of the biggest segments of the entertainment industry. But in a world without iPods or CD players, the only option was live music. So Solomon acquired his own singers so he could have them perform at his request.

Solomon would have grown up in a musical home. His father, David, was without equal as a hymn-writer and psalmist. So Solomon would have been well acquainted with the best music of his day. Interestingly, as king he was provided with a Levitical choir of priests made up exclusively of men (1 Chronicles 9:33). The mention of "female singers" indicates that Solomon had other choirs too. As king, he likely employed the most talented musicians from all over the land. But even with instant access to Israel's best music, Solomon found that true satisfaction was absent from the concert hall.

In our day, the entertainment industry has grown beyond music.

Film, television, radio, video games, and the Internet each offer various forms of electronic amusement. Technology has made these media instantly available for just about everyone. But whether it is the latest movie or the newest hit song, entertainment (in any form) cannot provide lasting happiness. If it could, last year's blockbuster would still be in theaters, and that favorite song would never get old—no matter how many times you listened to it.

Take it from Solomon, a man who never lacked for entertainment. He knew good music. For that matter, his popularity was such that he enjoyed the ultimate rock star status. Yet what was his take on it all? Entertainment might offer temporary escape, but it cannot give you lasting satisfaction.

Looking for Life in Romance (Ecclesiastes 2:8c)

When music wasn't enough, Solomon went looking for love. He openly confessed, "I provided for myself...the pleasures of men—many concubines" (2:8). First Kings 11:3 records, "He had seven hundred wives, princesses, and three hundred concubines, and his wives turned his heart away." With a thousand women at his beck and call, Solomon experienced romance and intimacy in fullness and variety. Yet these exploits not only failed to bring him lasting happiness (Ecclesiastes 2:11), they proved to be detrimental to his relationship with God (1 Kings 11:3).

The lie that sex and romance can bring ultimate satisfaction is still being told today. Romantic love, as wonderful as it is, is not the source of joy and fulfillment. If it were, divorce would be nonexistent and the phrase "happily ever after" would apply to every real-life romance, not just fairy tales. Men in particular are susceptible to sexual temptations—thinking they can find lasting pleasure by pursuing the lusts of their flesh. But nothing could be further from the truth. Solomon himself warned his son about the consequences of sexual sin in Proverbs 5. At the end of that chapter he wrote, "A man's ways are in full view of the LORD, and he examines all his paths. The evil deeds of a wicked man ensnare him; the cords of his sin hold him fast. He will die for lack of discipline, led astray by his own great folly" (verses 21-23 NIV). Sadly, Solomon did not always heed the warnings of his own fatherly advice.

Israel's third king had more romantic relationships than he knew what to do with. Yet they could not bring him lasting happiness. In fact, they got him into serious trouble with God (cf. 1 Kings 11:1-13). After searching for satisfaction in romance, Solomon's conclusion was the same as before: Ultimate fulfillment and joy can't be found there.

Looking for Life in Accomplishment (Ecclesiastes 2:9-11)

Solomon continued his search for satisfaction by taking stock of his own success. Perhaps human greatness was the key to happiness. As Solomon explained, "Then I became great and increased more than all who preceded me in Jerusalem...My heart was pleased because of all my labor and this was my reward for all my labor" (verses 9-10). After reviewing all of his accomplishments, Solomon was pretty impressed with himself. So much so that he claimed to be greater than any king before him, including his father David!

Solomon certainly had much to boast about, at least from a worldly perspective. He was so wealthy that silver "was not considered valuable in the days of Solomon" (1 Kings 10:22) because gold was available in such great supply. He was so wise that he "became greater than all the kings of the earth in riches and in wisdom" (1 Kings 10:23). He completed numerous building projects, including the Temple; had a magnificent army; and was the very icon of pomp and circumstance in the world of his day.

Yet even as Solomon looked at the greatness of his kingdom, noting all that he had accomplished, he saw how empty it all was. His conclusion is startling: "Thus I considered all my activities which my hands had done and the labor which I had exerted, and behold all was vanity and striving after wind and there was no profit under the sun" (verse 11). In spite of all he had done, Solomon realized that none of it could bring him lasting joy. His accomplishments, though impressive, brought him only temporary satisfaction.

What a reminder for those of us today who live in a world consumed by the American dream. We are told that we can accomplish anything we want if we just work hard enough, and then we will be happy and fulfilled. But does satisfaction await us at the top of the corporate ladder, or in the achievement of our goals and ambitions? Solomon's answer to that question is an unmistakable *no.* After a lifetime of amazing accomplishments, he came to the end of the rainbow expecting to find a treasure chest of happiness. But, as he himself testified, it was just a mirage.

Looking for Life in Wisdom (Ecclesiastes 2:12-17)

Solomon finished his quest for satisfaction by turning to the very wisdom God had given him. As he explained it, "So I turned to consider wisdom, madness and folly…And I saw that wisdom excels folly as light excels darkness. The wise man's eyes are in his head, but the fool walks in darkness" (verses 12-14). Perhaps, Solomon thought, he could find lasting joy in his own intellect. He was, after all, the wisest judge, the most esteemed philosopher, the most efficient administrator. Who can forget, for example, his insightful judgment regarding the two women who both claimed the same child (1 Kings 3:16-28)? Solomon's reputation for wisdom spread throughout the ancient Near East such that other rulers traveled to hear him speak and were astonished by the marvelous things he said (1 Kings 10:1-10).

But instead of applying his gift solely to matters of state and civic justice, Solomon used his unsurpassed creativity to chase after his lusts. Having found those pursuits empty, in desperation he turned to wisdom itself. Once again, rather than finding satisfaction and joy, he found pain and disappointment. In Ecclesiastes 1, he had already admitted that "in much wisdom there is much grief, and increasing knowledge results in increasing pain" (verse 18). Now he confessed that the vanity of his wisdom had caused him to despise his very existence. His conclusion is tragic and desperate: "So I hated life…because everything is futility and striving after wind" (2:17).

For the academic elite of our own day, Solomon's warning still rings true. A good education is a noble thing, but it cannot supply lasting satisfaction. Advanced degrees, philosophical sophistry, and intellectual pursuits are not the fountain of happiness. Solomon's wisdom was extraordinary; his IQ was literally off the charts. It went beyond human intellect because it was a gift from God Himself. Even so, devoid of God, Solomon found it to be empty. Like everything else he had tried, wisdom was not the answer to his problem.

SOLOMON'S FINAL WORDS

Solomon's pursuit of happiness ended in disappointment. Having searched for purpose, fulfillment, meaning, and joy, he found only restlessness, emptiness, confusion, and pain. Though he experimented with all of life's pleasures and pursuits—fun, alcohol, materialism, entertainment, romance, accomplishment, and wisdom—he found each of them wanting. They were all "futility and striving after wind."

So what can we learn from Solomon's failed experiment? For starters, we certainly know where *not* to look in our own search for satisfaction. Solomon has already done the hard part for us. He pursued worldly pleasures with far more gusto than we ever could. He had greater opportunity and greater resources. Even so, he discovered that the source of true happiness was not in any of the things he chased after. If we embrace Solomon's conclusion, we will be spared the emptiness that comes from pursuing the passing pleasures of this life.

But where is true happiness found?

Solomon gives us a clue in Ecclesiastes 2:24-25. There he explained, "I have seen that it is from the hand of God. For who can eat and who can have enjoyment without Him?" Solomon's rhetorical question points to the source of all true joy and fulfillment—namely, God Himself.

But in order to fully understand Solomon's conclusion, attention must be directed to the end of Ecclesiastes. The final chapter is where his ultimate answer and counsel is given. The verdict is no surprise: "'Vanity of vanities,' says the Preacher, 'all is vanity!'" (12:8). But as he penned the final words of the book, Solomon directed his readers to the true fount of lasting satisfaction. After 12 chapters of gloomy reflection, he ended with these words of hope: "The conclusion, when all has been heard, is: fear God and keep His commandments, because this applies to every person. For God will bring every act to judgment, everything which is hidden, whether it is good or evil" (12:13-14).

Herein is the real message. True meaning and satisfaction cannot be found in the pleasures of this world. But they are freely offered in the pleasures of God, revealed through His Word. Lasting happiness begins when we delight ourselves in the Lord, coming to Him with hearts full of worshipful obedience and reverential awe. Conversely, though we might pursue (and even obtain) all the things of this world, we will never be satisfied until we find our fulfillment in God and in His Son Jesus Christ. As Jesus Himself said, "I came that they may have life, and have it abundantly" (John 10:10). True life is found only in Him.

To be sure, God's creation is full of wonderful things that we can enjoy—from delicious food to breathtaking scenery to intimate friendships. The problem comes when we look to those earthly delights as the *source* of our happiness, rather than seeing them for what they truly are: marks on a compass that point to God. Only *He* can provide the lasting satisfaction we all desire. Thus, the joys of this life are truly meaningful only when God is at the center of our affections. They can be fully appreciated only when they are viewed from an eternal perspective and regulated by God's Word (Ecclesiastes 12:13-14). As Solomon himself stated in Ecclesiastes 11:9, "Rejoice, young man, during your childhood, and let your heart be pleasant during the days of young manhood. And follow the impulses of your heart and the desires of your eyes. Yet know that God will bring you to judgment for all these things."

Solomon's testimony serves as a somber warning and a timely reminder for us today. As he learned the hard way, the more we search for life outside of God, the more we will experience disappointment and emptiness within our hearts. Life lived apart from God is the height of vanity. But life lived in fellowship with Him is the sweetest and most fulfilling experience possible. Ironically, the wisest man who ever lived ended his search at the very place where we should begin ours: with the recognition that the pursuit of true happiness is the pursuit of God Himself.

Real Men Treasure God's Word
Lessons from the Life of Josiah

TOM PATTON

It was a beautiful evening in Southern California, just moments before our family was about to sit down for dinner. Out of nowhere my son Josiah came running to me in an unusually animated fashion. "What's this?" he asked, rubbing his hands up and down the black pebbled leather of an intriguing old volume he had found in our bookcase.

"Oh," I said, quickly recognizing what he held in his hands, "let's see what you have there." Reluctantly, as if he were handing over buried treasure, Josiah placed in my hands a most unique book. It wasn't just the fact that it was a Bible that made my son so curious. As a pastor, I've collected so many Bibles over the years that their presence in our home has become somewhat ubiquitous. No, what made this Bible special was the two inches of deep crimson color that encompassed its edges. Only the black spine was untouched by the dark red stain. It looked as if this Bible had been dipped in blood. I knew it was the book's fascinating appearance that had attracted my son to it. That's what had attracted me to it a lifetime before, when I first discovered it hidden between other books in my father's library.

"What we have here is an old Bible," I explained. "In fact, it's about one hundred and ten years old." "That's really ancient!" Josiah said with an astonished gulp. Smiling, I replied, "True, it's pretty old, but that's not what makes this Bible so special. What makes it special is its history." Then with both hands I carefully opened up its brittle cover to reveal three yellowed obituaries that had been delicately folded and placed inside the sleeve as a memorial. The bold-faced type on the first page revealed the name of the original owner. The obituary read, "The death of Reverend L.W. Swanner which occurred Sunday at 1:50 PM came as a severe shock to his many friends in this section. Deceased was 32 years of age at the time of his death…He was converted in 1897 [and] he gave his time, talent and strength to the Lord and His cause." As I read those words aloud, I could see my son's eyes growing large. He looked at me with unspoken wonder as I told him, "You've made a great discovery, Josiah, because this particular Bible belonged to your great-great grandfather. He was a follower of God, a faithful preacher, and a man who lived by the Book."

THE MOMENT OF FINDING THE BOOK

Almost 3000 years before that summer evening in California, an Israelite scribe named Shaphan raced excitedly into the presence of the most powerful man in Jerusalem. In his trembling hands he held an ancient scroll. His heart pounded as he carefully presented to King Josiah the treasure he had found. Moments earlier, the high priest Hilkiah had been directing the renovation of the Temple when he inadvertently discovered an old parchment nestled in a dark corner of a storage room. Knowing that any such discovery must be delivered at once to the administrative secretary, Hilkiah called for Shaphan to come evaluate the finding. It was by far the most mesmerizing relic Shaphan had ever seen; so much so that he quickly opened its binding and began to read. At once the entire weight of God's Word fell upon his mind and heart. In retrospect, nothing could have prepared him for what he read because no one in his entire generation had ever been exposed to what he now held in his hands. The Book of the Law had been lost, but now was found.

THE MYSTERY OF LOSING THE BOOK

As unimaginable as it may seem to our Bible-saturated modern culture, it is estimated that by the time the Scriptures were brought to King Josiah they had been lost for almost 100 years. The Word of God had not been read or followed for an entire generation! It had been neglected, forgotten, and lost.

How could this have happened? The answer is partly found in the relative scarcity of the Scriptures. In a day long before electronic duplication, no more than a few dozen copies of God's Word existed in Israel at any one time. Because they were written on fragile materials such as papyrus, leather, and parchment, the copies could easily disintegrate over the years and had to be preserved with the utmost care. But the chaos created by natural disasters and wars—which were especially frequent during the days of the divided kingdom—made their preservation a difficult challenge. To make matters worse, wicked rulers such as Manasseh were happy to see copies of God's law destroyed or, at least, put aside. The absence of God's Word made it easier for them to lead the people into idolatry and sin.

As tragic as it is unthinkable, after the death of the righteous King Hezekiah, the Word of God had been hidden away in the southern kingdom of Judah. Like a forgotten treasure it would not be rediscovered until a century later by a world that wasn't even looking for it. But everything changed when the Book found its way into the hands of King Josiah.

THE MAN WHO LAMENTED THE BOOK

According to 2 Chronicles 34:18, before Shaphan gave Josiah the scrolls, he read their entire contents to him. It must have been simultaneously exhilarating yet torturous for the young king to finally hear the law of God. Every word spoken pressed down heavy on his heart like a crushing hammer. This was God's standard, and Josiah realized it had gone completely ignored for nearly a century.

In response, the king grabbed his clothes and tore them in inde-
scribable anguish. He was cut to the quick—he was so deeply moved
by what he heard that he ripped his royal robe in horror and remorse.
For the first time in his life, he understood all that God demanded of
him. So he sat there motionless, overwhelmed with guilt and misery.
Then, in a decisive moment, he resolved to never let it happen again.
You see, once Josiah possessed the Word of God, he realized that the
Word of God must now possess him. He set out to change his entire
world, starting with the world within himself (2 Kings 23:3).

THE MEANING OF FINDING THE BOOK

We live in an era much like the days of Josiah. Though we have
plenty of Bibles, the Word of God has virtually been lost to our
society as well. Even in many churches the horrible truth is that the
Scriptures have been missing from the pulpit for a very long time.
The terrifying irony of Josiah's day can be seen in our day as well. The
Book of the Law wasn't lost in the marketplace, the universities, or
the public square. It was lost in the house of worship. The very place
from which it had once been hailed as the crown jewel of Jewish life
became the place it was hidden away.

Yet the story of Josiah gives us hope. Though the Word of God
had been lost in the Temple, it was also found there too. Oh that the
church today would rediscover the rich blessings of the Scriptures!
Like Josiah, we must all come face to face with the Book—to rediscover it once again, to tear our clothes in repentance, and to restore
it to its rightful place in our hearts, homes, and churches. That is
what it means to treasure God's Word.

THE METHOD OF FINDING THE BOOK

When we study the lives of the godly people in the Bible, we see
how the various events and stages of their lives slowly shaped their
character. Though Act One might reveal a degree of ignorance or

weakness in the person we are studying, ultimately we find that it was a necessary ingredient to prepare him for Act Two. Looking back at the entirety of a person's life allows us to see the full picture of God's providential handiwork—as He guided every event for His glory and the good of that person.

Such is certainly true of King Josiah. At the beginning of his life, he was ignorant of God's law. But that ignorance was the ingredient God used to fuel Josiah's desire to know the truth. And that desire, coupled with his discovery of God's Word, blossomed into a deep devotion to the Lord, which subsequently sparked a full-blown revival in Israel.

From desire to discovery to devotion, Josiah's commitment to the Word of God stands as a wonderful example for us to consider. Once he found the law of the Lord, his life was forever changed. His response to the Scriptures is notable. And it teaches us an important lesson—namely, that real men treasure God's Word. They are men of the Book. Let's look at three aspects of what that means.

1. Men of the Book Desire God's Word

Without question, King Josiah's greatest legacy is the spiritual reformation he brought to Judah. He was the sole restorer of God's Word to his generation and the single most powerful catalyst God used to revive His people. He understood the profound responsibility he possessed to take the newly discovered Book of Truth back to the people, returning it to its rightful place. But that could not have happened if Josiah did not desire to obey the Word of God.

When Josiah ascended the throne of Israel, he was only eight years old. It was a time of great spiritual darkness in Israel. Josiah's godless father, before being assassinated, had tried to wipe out worship of the true God. The prophets Isaiah and Micah were dead, and Jeremiah was not yet on the scene. The law of God had been lost, which meant Josiah did not even have access to the truth of Scripture. And yet, in the eighth year of his reign, at age 16, Josiah "began to seek the God of his father David; and in the twelfth year he began to purge Judah and Jerusalem of the high places, the Asherim, the carved images and the molten images" (2 Chronicles 34:3).

In the midst of the pagan influences of idolatry, in spite of the suppression of the Scriptures, young Josiah sought the Lord! And by grace the Lord gave Josiah enough light to come to know Him. We cannot be sure how this happened. Perhaps through a secret meeting with a worshiper of Yahweh, or maybe through finding a small portion of Scripture that had not been lost. We just don't know. But somehow the Lord led Josiah to Himself. And four years later, the king began to bring about reform (2 Chronicles 34:3-7).

Even without a copy of God's law in hand, Josiah knew enough to destroy every idol (2 Chronicles 34:7) and renovate the Temple for worship (verse 8). And yet though he had an overwhelming zeal for God, he still didn't have the Book. The best he could do was direct his efforts toward the things he thought needed to change. But he had no blueprint; he lacked a biblical pattern of counsel to follow.

Nonetheless, his desire was a noble one—to honor God and clear out anything that might distract from pure worship. Though he did not yet possess the sacred scrolls, he clearly possessed a desire to know and obey the Word of God. Like Josiah, if we are to *treasure* God's Word we must first *desire* it. The apostle Peter gave that very instruction to the Christians in Asia Minor, commanding them to "long for the pure milk of the word, so that by it you may grow in respect to salvation" (1 Peter 2:2). If we hope to grow in godliness and spiritual maturity, our longing must precede our living.

2. Men of the Book Discover God's Word

In addition to desiring God's Word, godly men must discover it as well. Churches today are full of men who have placed their faith in Christ yet base their daily decisions on something other than the Word of Christ. They want to know the will of God, but they fail to look to the Word of God for themselves. Following the example of Josiah, we need to blow the dust off of our unopened Bibles and discover its life-giving truth all over again. Once Josiah found the Book of the Law, he responded with repentance and resolve. He sprang into action, determined to lead the nation in keeping with God's Word.

According to Deuteronomy 31:26 the original copy of the law, which was penned by Moses, was deposited beside the ark of the covenant and kept there to be read every seven years (cf. verses 10-11). Interestingly, there were no provisions in Scripture for making copies until the time that Israel had a king. So for an undisclosed period of time there were no copies of the Scriptures being made at all. But in Deuteronomy 17:18 we read, "Now it shall come about when he [the king] sits on the throne of his kingdom, he shall write for himself a copy of this law on a scroll in the presence of the Levitical priests." In other words, it was the responsibility of the king to make a copy of the Scriptures for himself.

Perhaps there were copies made for the prophets or priests, but the point was that if the king were to lead God's people rightly he needed his own copy of God's Word. In order to fully comprehend what the divine King required, the human king must have direct access to the Book. He would need to study it, bury it in his heart, meditate on its beauty, remember its mandates, and teach its epic lessons. But since the time of Hezekiah, a century before Josiah, no such copies had been made. The result was spiritually disastrous for the kingdom of Judah.

The devastating effects were visibly evident at the Temple, which by Josiah's time had not been repaired for at least 60 years (and maybe as many as 200 years). Sadly, as the biblical record indicates, "the kings of Judah had let [it] go to ruin" (2 Chronicles 34:11). But King Josiah, desiring to do what was right before the Lord, made plans to restore it. After his renovations began, it would still be several years before a copy of the law was discovered. And when it was found, everything changed.

That's why Josiah trembled with so much anticipation when Shaphan rushed into the throne room and announced what had been found. That is also why the king tore his royal robes as he heard the Word of God being read—he came to realize just how far astray Judah had gone. Josiah's response was humble and heartfelt: "Great is the wrath of the LORD which is poured out on us because our fathers have not observed the word of the LORD, to do according to all that is written in this book" (verse 21). And God heard his cry of reverent repentance (verses 26-28).

Josiah wanted to do the right thing but he didn't have the instruction manual—until now. Once he found the Book, he realized that his best intentions had been insufficient because they had not been guided by the Word of truth. So it is with us. Unless we are living by the Book, our best efforts are in vain. Like Josiah, we must discover God's Word for ourselves.

3. Men of the Book Devour God's Word

As Josiah imbibed the Scriptures, he learned that there was much to do. Renovation was required not only for the Temple's structure, but for the very way in which worship was conducted in Judah. So what did the king do? He devoured the Book, carefully paying attention to every detail. Then he shared his incredible findings with everyone around him. According to 2 Chronicles 34:30, he "went up to the house of the LORD and all the men of Judah, the inhabitants of Jerusalem, the priests, the Levites and all the people, from the greatest to the least; and he read in their hearing all the words of the book of the covenant which was found in the house of the LORD." He personally tasted of its rich truth, and then he publicly proclaimed it to the nation.

Moreover, Josiah was quick to apply its precepts. Once he understood what God required, he did not hesitate to obey. He reinstated the long-neglected Passover and contributed 30,000 lambs and 3000 bulls from his own flocks as sacrifices for the people to offer unto the Lord. Second Chronicles 35:18 explains that "there had not been celebrated a Passover like it in Israel since the days of Samuel the prophet; nor had any of the kings of Israel celebrated such a Passover as Josiah did with the priests, the Levites, all Judah and Israel who were present, and the inhabitants of Jerusalem." He was so moved by what he read that, having devoured the truth, he sparked revival across the entire nation. So it is with us. Once we discover God's Word for ourselves, devoting our hearts and minds to its truth, we must respond in obedient action.

Second Kings 23:25 gives a glowing report about Josiah's life: "Before him there was no king like him who turned to the LORD with all his heart and with all his soul and with all his might, according to all the law of Moses; nor did any like him arise after him." What a legacy! In all of Judah's history, no king displayed a deeper commitment to turning away from error and submissively obeying the Word of God than Josiah. Thus he stands as a wonderful model of the reformation and revival that comes when the Scriptures are desired, discovered, and devoured. King Josiah's story is both unique and compelling, warning us of the dangers that can come when the Scriptures are forgotten, and reminding us of our need to treasure God's Word with all our hearts. If we do, we will share in Josiah's legacy—influencing our friends and families toward godliness and leaving a wonderful heritage of blessing for generations to come.

TREASURING THE WORD OF GOD

During one of the chapel sessions I attended while I was in seminary, our school president preached a message on the importance of God's Word from Psalm 19. During the message he spoke about a very large, sixteenth-century Bible that he had seen and held. Upon opening it, he explained, the first thing he noticed was that every page had been stained. It was obvious that, at some point in the past, the Bible had been submerged into liquid about three quarters of the way up. But this was not just any liquid. The waterline on each page had faded some, but the reddish-pink hue was still discernable.

We sat there silently, amazed as he went on to explain the historical context. In the early sixteenth century, Bloody Mary—the Catholic Queen of England—massacred hundreds of Protestant Christians. Owning a Bible was illegal, as was believing the true gospel. In some cases, before a person was burned at the stake, his wrists were slit and placed over a bowl into which his blood would pour. Then his accusers would take his Bible and, as an act of contempt and disdain, dip it into the crimson pool.

The result was a volume of blood-stained pages. But what was originally intended as a mockery now stood as a monument to the faithfulness of the martyrs. As our president finished his message, speaking to a room full of men training for pastoral ministry, he challenged us to never forget the price that some have paid for the Scriptures. To the martyrs of the sixteenth century, the Word of God was precious. They treasured God's Word—so much so that they were willing to bleed and die for it. *Are we?*

Dinnertime was over and so was my discussion. I handed my great-grandfather's old Bible back to my son, Josiah. Though I knew he was very perceptive for an eight-year-old boy, I thought maybe it would be good for him to stand there for just a moment holding that Bible and allowing all I had said to sink in. I was sure the crimson-rimmed book felt a little different now in his hands, most likely a whole lot heavier. Then, almost like I was conducting a rite-of-passage ceremony, I told him, "Go ahead and put it back on the shelf, but be careful Josiah. That's not just any book you've found. To our family that's a treasure."

4

Real Men Pray with Boldness
Lessons from the Life of Elijah

JUSTIN McKITTERICK

The dust from a land dying of thirst finally began to settle after a long day. The colorless countryside had not tasted rain for over three years. Drought smothered the land and as a result, famine plagued the living. A tired prophet, accompanied only by a servant, hiked the last painful steps to reach the top of Mount Carmel, only to fall to his knees. Though exhausted, he did not crouch down to find physical rest. A greater need burdened his soul. He knelt to pray. Bowed low, with his face between his knees, Elijah boldly petitioned the Creator of the universe for relief.

WHERE ARE THE PRAYING MEN OF OUR DAY?

As we consider the example of Elijah, a question immediately arises: Where are the men of our generation who, like that notable prophet, are marked by humble yet confident prayerfulness? Sadly, we live in a time when prayer is talked about much more than it is actually practiced. But where are the men with calloused knees and tender hearts? How easy it is to feel conviction over our prayerlessness and yet do nothing to change. Too often, we are content with halfhearted requests uttered as we drift off to sleep instead of enjoying the awesome privilege of deep communion with God Himself.

J.C. Ryle said, "Tell me what a man's prayers are, and I will soon tell you the state of his soul."[1] We often wonder why there are so many struggling souls—why the hearts of men are so easily distracted, discouraged, and deceived. Ryle's potent words reveal the need for us to pray. The health of our hearts and souls is dependent upon it. Prayer gives access to the throne room of grace, where we are invited to come with humble reverence and bold confidence (Hebrews 4:16). Prayer in accordance with God's Word allows His will to pervade our hearts and His glory to consume our minds.

James wrote, "The effective prayer of a righteous man can accomplish much" (James 5:16). As righteous men pray, their petitions rise like incense before the Lord—and He is pleased to answer them. In fact, within God's sovereign purposes and according to His infinite wisdom, He uses prayer to accomplish His plans. To be clear, the power of prayer is not in the man who prays, but in the God who answers. It "can accomplish much" only because God can do "far more abundantly beyond all that we ask or think" (Ephesians 3:20). And our great God delights in the prayers of His people—those who love Him and walk in righteousness (cf. Psalm 145:18-19).

Elijah was such a man. In James 5:17-18, he is presented as a model of powerful prayer. But what made his prayer life so effective? And what can we learn from this man about the way we should pray? In order to answer these questions, we need to dig deeper into the life and ministry of this faithful man of God.

A TIME OF SPIRITUAL DROUGHT

Elijah arrived on the scene during one of Israel's darkest hours. Civil war had split the nation in two. Idol worship ran rampant and the ways of God had been forgotten. Generations of wicked monarchs had left the people spiritually destitute. The times were so discouraging that even Elijah wondered if he was the only true believer left (1 Kings 19:14). The religious landscape of the day was barren and parched.

Ahab, the ruler of the northern kingdom, was the most corrupt monarch in Israel's history up to that time. According to 1 Kings 16:33, "Ahab did more to provoke the LORD God of Israel than all the kings of Israel who were before him." Like lethal venom, his reign poisoned Israel with godlessness.

Ahab's wickedness was surpassed only by that of his wife. He married the Baal-worshiping Jezebel, a daughter of the Phoenician king of the Sidonians. The idolatrous worship of Baal was common among Israel's neighbors, and Jezebel brought it with her when she became queen. If Ahab was the poisonous venom infecting Israel, Jezebel was the snake behind the bite. Scripture records that "there was never a man like Ahab, who sold himself to do evil in the eyes of the LORD, *urged on by Jezebel his wife*" (1 Kings 21:25 NIV, emphasis added). Jezebel's idolatry swayed Ahab like a riptide controls a rudderless boat, and the rest of Israel came along for the disastrous ride. It was in the midst of this downward spiral of sin that God called Elijah to a ministry of confrontation.

Israel's idolatry was a serious offense to God. Centuries earlier, Moses had warned the people about the severe consequences of false worship.

> Beware that your hearts are not deceived, and that you do not turn away and serve other gods and worship them. Or the anger of the LORD will be kindled against you, and He will shut up the heavens so that there will be no rain and the ground will not yield its fruit; and you will perish quickly from the good land which the LORD is giving you (Deuteronomy 11:16-17).

Israel, like any agricultural society, depended on rain for its fruitfulness. Without precipitation, the land quickly became lifeless dust. Elijah knew well the words of God revealed through Moses. The Lord had warned that spiritual drought would bring physical drought. Now Elijah prayed that God's promised punishment would be realized. We learn from James that "he prayed earnestly that it would not rain, and it did not rain on the earth for three years and six months. Then he prayed again, and the sky poured rain and the earth produced its fruit" (James 5:17-18).

When Elijah approached Ahab to tell him of the coming drought, the ground had already been dry for six months. The normal dry season had come and gone. It was time for rain, but as Elijah's foreboding prophecy made clear, rain would not come. Ahab must have been shocked by the prophet's bold prediction: "Surely there shall be neither dew nor rain these years, except by my word" (1 Kings 17:1). Not a drop of water would touch the ground of Israel for three years—until the day Elijah climbed to the top of Mount Carmel and knelt to pray for rain.

Some 900 years later, James looked back to Elijah's prayer life as a model for how we should pray. Elijah knew the Word of God, and he prayed accordingly. His bold confidence was not placed in himself, but in the promises and person of God. He asked God to stop the rain because he remembered the warnings revealed through Moses and because he had a passion that the Lord alone be worshiped. His fervent prayer life, informed by Scripture and consumed by God's glory, makes him a compelling example for us to emulate.

BOLD PRAYERS FROM A NORMAL MAN

At this point, it is easy to feel intimidated. Elijah is one of the spiritual superstars of the Bible. He is considered one of the greatest prophets and is renowned for his powerful miracles, such as raising a widow's son from the dead (1 Kings 17:17-24), calling down fire from heaven (1 Kings 18:36-38), and dividing the waters of the Jordan (2 Kings 2:8). His bold denunciation of Israel's sin makes him seem fearless. And his fiery chariot ride to heaven almost makes him sound legendary (2 Kings 2:11). His legacy is such that the New Testament mentions him 29 times. He even appeared with Jesus at the Transfiguration and many believe he will minister on earth again during the Tribulation. This man is a spiritual all-star.

I can hear your thoughts already. *I appreciate the apostle James pointing to Elijah as an example, but this guy is out of my league. He was a prophet sent by God and he was the real deal. He performed miracles and spoke the word of God. The man didn't even die. How am I supposed to relate to him?* But before you discount Elijah as an impossible standard, look again at the amazing statement in James 5:17: "Elijah was a man with a nature like ours."

Elijah was a very godly man, but he was still only a man. According to James' description, he had desires, struggles, and a nature like ours. He was righteous, but not perfect. He was used by God in great ways, but he was a normal human being just like you and me. He got hungry (1 Kings 17:11) and tired (1 Kings 19:5). He struggled with fear, anxiety, uncertainty, and even depression (1 Kings 19:3-4). He was criticized (1 Kings 17:18) and at times felt all alone (1 Kings 19:14). When Jezebel tried to kill him, Elijah ran away in fear, hid in the wilderness, and wallowed in despair (1 Kings 19:4). He knew pain and hardship, and he was subject to the same temptations, distractions, burdens, and excuses that we face. Yet through the adversity, uncertainty, and struggle, Elijah was faithful to pray. As William Varner observed, "You see, that's the difference between Elijah and us. It's not that his nature was different than ours; it's that we have not learned to pray like he prayed. That's the difference. He was a man, but he was a man who stood in the presence of God."[2]

It is significant to notice that James did not call us to imitate Elijah's prophetic duties. He did not focus on Elijah's miracles or his confrontation with Ahab. Nothing in Scripture instructs us to try and duplicate the supernatural wonders Elijah performed. But we are called to imitate his prayer life. James purposely emphasized the fact that Elijah was a normal man, a man just like us, who offered up bold prayers in faith.

THE PREREQUISITES OF PRAYER:
FAITH AND RIGHTEOUSNESS

It may seem odd to suggest there are prerequisites to prayer, but the boldness and effectiveness of Elijah's prayer life was built upon a strong spiritual foundation of faith and righteousness.

First, let's consider Elijah's faith. At the beginning of his letter, James wrote,

> If any of you lacks wisdom, let him ask of God, who gives to all generously and without reproach, and it will be given to him. But he *must ask in faith without any doubting*, for the one who doubts is like the surf of the sea, driven and tossed by the wind. For that man ought not to expect that he will receive anything from the Lord, being a double-minded man, unstable in all his ways (James 1:5-8, emphasis added).

Without faith, prayer is pointless. Prayer acknowledges the power, sovereignty, and sufficiency of God. It admits human weakness and depends on divine wisdom and strength. When Elijah prayed, he believed God could and would answer. Though his circumstances were difficult, emotional, and uncertain, Elijah prayed with faith that the all-wise and all-powerful God would hear and respond.

When Elijah asked God to close up the skies, he prayed in faith knowing God would also open them again. After three-and-a-half years had passed, he climbed to the top of Mount Carmel and even though there was not a cloud in the sky, he prayed for rain. His faith was so strong that even before he started to pray he told Ahab there would be "the sound of the roar of a heavy shower" (1 Kings 18:41). While on his knees, Elijah sent his servant to look toward the sea for any sign of coming moisture. Six different times the servant came back and reported, "There is nothing." Elijah's faith was not deterred. He continued to pray. When the servant returned the seventh time, there was a new look on his face. "Behold, a cloud as small as a man's hand is coming up from the sea" (1 Kings 19:44). Soon the downpour began.

Though Elijah is not specifically named in Hebrews 11, he was certainly characterized by the same confident faith that marked Abel, Enoch, Noah, Abraham, and all the rest who are listed there. As the writer of Hebrews noted, "Faith is the assurance of things hoped for, the conviction of things not seen. For by it the men of old gained approval" (verses 1-2). Elijah placed his hope in the Lord even when the answer he sought was unseen from an earthly perspective. His unwavering confidence in God's word and in God's power enabled him to pray with boldness.

James described Elijah not only as a man of faith, but also as a man of righteousness. Speaking of Elijah, he wrote, "The effective prayer of *a righteous man* can accomplish much" (James 1:16, emphasis added). James understood that sin and prayer do not mix. So he reminded his readers that a holy life is essential to effective prayer.

If you've ever driven a car with a flat tire, you know how difficult it is to control where the car is going under such circumstances. The car is quickly pulled and tugged off course. Even slowing down does not solve the problem. Ultimately, the only thing you can do is stop. Nothing slows down the power of prayer faster than sin. Like a flat tire, sin pulls your heart and mind off course, taking you out of God's will and putting you at odds with His holiness. Put simply, sin inhibits prayer. Psalm 66:18 makes the point crystal clear: "If I regard iniquity in my heart, the Lord will not hear me" (kjv). On the other hand, though, "the Lord...hears the prayer of the righteous" (Proverbs 15:29).

The fact is, you cannot pray with confidence if you are living in unrepentant sin. This does not mean perfection is required. All of us, including Elijah, are sinners saved by grace who continually grow in sanctification. But only as we confess our sins and walk in holiness, knowing that we have been forgiven through Jesus Christ, can we come boldly before the throne of grace.

A PATTERN FOR POWERFUL PRAYER

The book of James invites us to learn from Elijah's example. We might not pray for rain, but we are called to pray with the same fervency as Elijah, expecting God to work in accordance with His word for His glory. With the prerequisites of faith and righteousness in mind, we can now turn our attention to the specifics of the prophet's prayer life. Elijah modeled at least four characteristics of powerful prayer that we would do well to imitate. As we study his example, we quickly learn what it looks like when real men pray.

1. Men of Prayer Pray Earnestly

James 5:17 explains that Elijah "prayed earnestly." The literal translation of that statement reads, "with prayer, he prayed." The language is emphatic and reveals the intensity of Elijah's intercession. He specifically and intentionally devoted himself to prayer. Surely he felt the heart-wrenching weight of his request for divine judgment to fall on Israel. But he was also consumed with reverential awe for the One whom he served, and he was more concerned with God's glory than anything else. If things in Israel were to change, the Lord would have to do it. And so, the prophet fell to his knees and prayed. Prayer was not a trivial afterthought or a backup plan; it was Elijah's only plan because God was his only hope.

Oh that we would approach God with that same level of intensity! How much more intently we would pray if only we would remember how great God is, how weak we are, how lost the world is, and how much is at stake. We need to remind ourselves of Paul's exhortation, "Devote yourselves to prayer, keeping alert in it with an attitude of thanksgiving" (Colossians 4:2). Earnest prayer does not just happen. It takes effort, focus, and time. Like an aspiring athlete who prioritizes hard work in the gym, the man of God devotes himself to prayer. He understands that his spiritual vitality depends on it.

2. Men of Prayer Pray Frequently

We often relegate prayer to our private devotions. As Christians we desperately need those times, but for Elijah prayer went beyond that. It was not consigned to a daily to-do list, compartmentalized to a quiet time, or reduced to a few short words before a meal. For Elijah, prayer was a lifestyle. In 1 Thessalonians 5:17, Paul instructed believers to "pray without ceasing," and Elijah modeled that principle.

Prayer saturated the prophet's life. When he wanted God to send a drought, he prayed. When the widow's son died, he prayed. When he confronted the prophets of Baal on Mount Carmel, he prayed. When he told Ahab that God would send rain, he prayed. When Jezebel murderously sought his life, he prayed. He prayed publicly on the mountaintop and privately in the desert. Wherever he went, whatever his circumstances, Elijah lived in constant communion with God. There is much for us to learn in this regard. Elijah's boldness before the Lord came because he was frequently in intimate fellowship with Him.

Prayer is a wonderful part of the relationship believers enjoy with God. It is a natural outgrowth of our fellowship with Him, and thus should be a normal part of our everyday lives. Because it is a lifestyle, the Bible does not give a standardized formula for when to pray. It simply assumes that godly men are characterized by prayerfulness. We see David praying early in the morning (Psalm 5:3) and late at night (Psalm 63:6). Daniel prayed three times each day (Daniel 6:10). Jesus often slipped away into the quietness of the wilderness to pray alone (Luke 5:16). Nehemiah uttered a quick prayer for help when he stood before the king (Nehemiah 2:4). Paul prayed night and day for the Thessalonians (1 Thessalonians 3:10). As these examples demonstrate, the expectation of Scripture is that godly men pray persistently and regularly—not motivated by vain repetition or a rigid routine, but by a heart that truly loves to commune with the living God.

3. Men of Prayer Pray Humbly

James 4:6 reports that "God is opposed to the proud, but gives grace to the humble." Elijah's prayer life was characterized by humility. When the prophet prayed for rain, he "crouched down on the earth and put his face between his knees" (1 Kings 18:42). His reverent posture reflected the humility within his heart. He did not draw near to God casually or flippantly. He approached God with confidence, but not arrogance.

Another vivid example of Elijah's humility in prayer is revealed in 1 Kings 18:36-37. After the priests of Baal failed to call down fire from heaven with the help of their false gods, it was Elijah's turn to boldly appeal to the true God. Notice the purpose behind his request:

> O LORD, the God of Abraham, Isaac and Israel, today let it be known that You are God in Israel and that I am Your servant and I have done these things at Your word. Answer me, O LORD, answer me, that this people may know that You, O LORD, are God, and that you have turned their heart back again.

Elijah prayed that God's name would be known and that His glory would be seen among the people. His motivation was not to make a name for himself. If he was to be identified at all, it was only as the Lord's servant. His sole concern was the vindication and honor of God.

Elijah's humble disposition provides us with a much-needed

challenge. Often our prayers are ineffective because we are more concerned about our own wishes than we are about God's glory. But His praise should be the ultimate purpose of our prayers. His will should be the longing of our hearts. Like our Savior, we should approach our heavenly Father with words of humble submission: "Not as I will, but as You will" (Matthew 26:39). When we do, we will be able to echo the words of the psalmist: "Not to us, O Lord, not to us, but to Your name give glory" (Psalm 115:1).

4. Men of Prayer Pray Boldly

Elijah's words on Mount Carmel ring with confident passion: "Answer me, O Lord, answer me" (1 Kings 18:37). When was the last time you prayed like that? Elijah approached God with boldness and tenacity. He expected God to answer his prayers—not out of presumption but out of genuine faith.

Elijah approached God with boldness for several reasons. First, he knew God's Word and he aligned his prayers accordingly. Second, he prayed for God's glory. Elijah's sole concern was that God's reputation would be vindicated. Third, Elijah expected remarkable answers because he knew the One to whom he was praying—the all-powerful Creator. The nature of our prayers is directly related to our understanding of who God is. Fourth, simply stated, Elijah was willing to ask. James 4:2 states, "You do not have because you do not ask." The simplicity of that statement is sobering. Often we do not enjoy the blessings of answered prayer because we do not pray in the first place. Jesus' words to His disciples should encourage and challenge us with regard to how boldly we pray: "If you ask Me anything in My name, I will do it" (John 14:14). What a promise! Prayers offered according to His will and for His glory will certainly be answered.

Those who remember God's Word, know His character, and seek His glory will inevitably pray with confident faith. Like Elijah, they trust in His infinite wisdom, rely on His eternal power, and rest in

His fatherly love. No matter what their circumstances, they pray earnestly, frequently, humbly, and boldly—knowing that their sovereign Lord has everything under control. He is the living God, and unlike Baal, He hears the prayers of His children. What a comfort that is for those who walk with Him!

As we reflect on the prayer life of Elijah, let's leave behind the shallows of doubt and inconsistency, and instead swim boldly in the depths of confident faith and joyous fellowship with God.

Real Men Love to Worship

Lessons from the Hymn Writers of Israel

JOHN MARTIN

I didn't like the worship," one man said to me after I asked him why he changed churches. "The preaching was pretty good and the people were friendly, but the worship wasn't for me."

Sound familiar? The terms *worship* and *music* have, unfortunately, become synonymous in the contemporary church. A civil war rages over what style of music churches should use, with a sense that the wrong choice will somehow limit a congregation's ability to worship God. The result is more and more churches splitting over the "worship."

Now, I love music! As a musician, my life is filled with music. But *worship* is much more than *music*. Music, in and of itself, does not produce worship. It has no inherent spiritual property. Rather, music is an expression of our worship. Music is a tool—a wonderful vehicle God has given to us through which we can express our praise.

So what is worship? Paul tells us in Romans 12:1-2 that worship is a spiritual service to God. It is the wholehearted response of a soul captivated by the wonder of God's mercies. And as we will see in the Psalms, the more we know Him the greater our worshipful response will be, whether or not there is any instrumental accompaniment.

Worship, then, encompasses all of life as we *first* present ourselves wholly to God through Christ, day by day, moment by moment—and *then* as we sing. Or as David put it, "My heart is steadfast, O God, my heart is steadfast; I will sing, yes, I will sing praises!" (Psalm 57:7). Singing is the result of a heart that is resolutely focused on God.

MEET THE HYMN WRITERS OF ISRAEL

The book of Psalms is a collection of praises, prayers, and meditations penned by a handful of authors, including David, Asaph, Moses, Ethan, and the sons of Korah. They are rich expressions of worship written out of significant personal experiences and trials. We see the full range of human emotions in the Psalms, from the highest joys to the deepest moments of despair—often in the same passage. But one thing is consistent and clear: The writers exhibit unyielding worship grounded in the knowledge of God.

Though the theme of worship occurs repeatedly throughout the book of Psalms, we will look at five specific passages, finding in each a characteristic of true worship. As we do, we'll learn that worship is more than just singing on Sundays, it is a way of life. It often results in singing (Ephesians 5:19-20), but it can find expression in any area of our lives. As Paul told the Corinthians, "Whether, then, you eat or drink or whatever you do, do all to the glory of God" (1 Corinthians 10:31). The psalmists were real men who experienced real triumphs and real trials. Through it all, their worshipful responses stand as a wonderful example to us and as a compelling reminder that—no matter what our circumstances—real men love to worship God.

1. *True Worship Longs for Fellowship with God (Psalm 84)*

For the psalmists, the Temple in Jerusalem was the most desirable place on earth. No place and no pleasure could compare with the blessing of being in those sacred courts. There in the Holy of

Holies was the manifest presence of God—the Shekinah glory. And although earth, "heaven and the highest heaven cannot contain [Him]" (1 Kings 8:27), the Lord was pleased, in a sense, to make the Temple His dwelling place. So, for the Israelite, to worship at the Temple was to know the high joy of communing with the living God.

Psalm 84 gives us the picture of a man whose all-consuming desire was to be found in the courts of the Lord. He was homesick for the place where his "heart and flesh sing for joy to the living God" (verse 2). But for some reason he found himself separated from the Temple. Perhaps he was traveling, or maybe he was ill. Whatever the cause, it was a painful separation.

And so, unable to contain his affections, the writer breaks forth with words of intense longing: "How lovely are Your dwelling places, O LORD of hosts! My soul longed and even yearned for the courts of the LORD" (verse 1). The Temple was a beautiful building, but the writer was not complimenting its architecture or décor. No, he was thinking of the wonderful fellowship he enjoyed with the Lord in the house where God dwelt. That was the place he longed and even yearned to be.

This deep, visceral longing was so intense that it consumed his whole being—his soul, heart, and flesh (verse 2). He found himself envying the birds that nested near the Temple (verse 3). And if the birds were privileged, how much more the priests who ministered in God's house "ever praising" Him (verse 4). With every beat of his heart, the psalmist longed to worship there.

Having experienced the transcendent beauty of God's presence, the psalmist was so consumed with it that he desperately wanted more. He could not wait until he would come to the Temple once again. He had seen all that sin had to offer, and his conclusion was that nothing could compare to the soul-satisfying joy of fellowship with God. And so his anthem resounded with these words: "A day in Your courts is better than a thousand outside. I would rather stand at the threshold of the house of my God than dwell in the tents of wickedness. For the LORD God is a sun and shield; the LORD gives grace and glory; no good thing does He withhold from those who walk uprightly" (verses 10-11).

In those two verses the psalmist teaches us an important lesson—namely, that true fellowship with God is immeasurably greater and more satisfying than any sinful pleasure. Sin promises satisfaction, but only God can provide it. In fact, the more we know and worship God, the more satisfied we become in Him. And when we are satisfied in Him, He is glorified and worshiped. As Jonathan Edwards explained, "The happiness of the creature consists in rejoicing in God, by which also God is magnified and exalted."[1] Or, as John Piper has said, "God is most glorified in us, when we are most satisfied in Him."[2]

2. *True Worship Seeks Satisfaction in the Lord (Psalm 63)*

Psalm 63 echoes the theme that true satisfaction is found in God alone. In a moment of great honesty, the author (David) acknowledged his utter dependency on God. Though he was being hunted by Saul and forced to hide in the wilderness (1 Samuel 22), David knew he could find refuge in the Lord (Psalm 63:9-11). Yet his primary concern was not his immediate circumstances. Rather, like the writer of Psalm 84, David was troubled by the fact that he was separated from the dwelling place of God (verse 2).

David began by crying out, "O God, You are my God; I shall seek you earnestly; my soul thirsts for You, my flesh yearns for You, in a dry and weary land where there is no water" (verse 1). His words are full of worship, and they express the longing of his whole being—*soul* and *flesh*. David was not describing his literal surroundings, though he was hiding in the desert. Rather, he was describing his spiritual thirst—a longing he knew only God could satisfy.

He continued with words of praise: "Because Your lovingkindness is better than life, my lips will praise You. So I will bless You as long as I live; I will lift up my hands in Your name" (verses 3-4). In just a few short phrases, David teaches us volumes about worship. Why should our lips praise God? Why should we worship Him for as long as we live? It is not because of our circumstances, but rather because He deserves to be worshiped no matter what our circumstances might be. After all, His lovingkindness is better than life itself! Even in our darkest trials God is still worthy of our praise. He is our hope, our refuge, and our satisfaction. Martin Luther said it this way: "Let [the world] trust and glory in their wisdom, their might, their wealth, and their possessions, my heart triumphs in the living God."[3]

Search your heart. What does it long for? What is your attitude toward worship? Is your vision of God so great and so satisfying that you cannot help but overflow with thanksgiving and praise? If we do not long to worship God, it is inevitably because something other than God has become great in our eyes. Psalm 16:11 says of God, "In Your presence is fullness of joy; in Your right hand there are pleasures forever." When we fail to fully delight in Him, we rob ourselves of the *fullness of joy*. Find satisfaction in God alone. Seek Him with your whole heart. Then He will be glorified and you will be able to sing with the psalmist, "O God, You are my God...My soul is satisfied" (Psalm 63:1,5).

3. True Worship Persists Through Difficult Times (Psalm 27)

The book of Psalms is filled with examples of real men who worshipped in and through difficult circumstances. We can empathize with them. Like us, they had fears, needs, difficulties, and weaknesses. Yet they never stopped looking to God in hope and praise. Even in the face of uncertainty, they worshiped the Lord without wavering.

Psalm 27 is the personal account of David as he faced yet another trial. In this heartfelt passage, we find an exemplary response to extreme uncertainty. Yet the purpose of this psalm is not to draw attention to David, but to God, as it teaches us to worship even in the midst of tribulation.

David was on the run. His enemies were malicious "evildoers" who wanted him dead. He described them as wild animals eager to devour his flesh (verse 2) and bring him to a violent end (verse 12). But how did David respond to the imminent danger? Did he question God? No, he did just the opposite. He worshiped Him! With words of praise, he sang, "The LORD is my light and my salvation; whom shall I fear? The LORD is the defense of my life" (verse 1). His faith in God allowed him to ask, "Whom shall I dread?" After all, he exclaimed, "Though a host encamp against me, my heart will not fear; though war rise against me, in spite of this I shall be confident" (verse 3). David did not fear the uncertain circumstances of life because his hope was grounded in the unchanging character of God. David knew he could not put his trust in any other source. "I would have despaired," he wrote, "unless I had believed that I would see the goodness of the LORD" (verse 13). This spirit of joyful assurance caused him to "sing praises" (verse 6). The Lord alone was his "light and [his] salvation" (verse 1).

In verses 7-12, we see that David's confidence in God resulted in his humble supplication, during which he poured out his heart to the Lord. Holding nothing back, he pleaded with God, "Hear, O LORD, when I cry with my voice, and be gracious to me and answer me" (verse 7). In verse 13, he ended his requests with the same quiet certainty that had preceded them: "I will see the LORD's goodness in the land of the living" (HCSB). David was confident that, before he died, he would see the Lord's goodness displayed in his trial. And, in a moment of preaching to himself, he gave us this final exhortation: "Wait for the LORD; be strong and let your heart take courage; yes, wait for the LORD" (verse 14).

The questions that arise from David's example are both penetrating and practical. How are you responding to the stresses and trials of life? Are you confident in God's goodness? Are you worshiping?

As men, we tend to respond to difficulty with an attitude of self-sufficiency. But that never goes well. Even our best efforts will end in failure and frustration. The right response is to look to the Lord. It is not enough to simply "be strong and let your heart take courage" (verse 14). That is a meaningless exhortation apart from the rest of the verse: "Wait for the Lord...yes, wait for the Lord."

Real men love to worship even in the midst of trials. Or perhaps a better way of putting it is this: Real men love to worship *especially* in the midst of trials. We do not have to endure hardship in our own strength. Rather, God invites us to bare our hearts before Him, acknowledging our insufficiency and trusting in His goodness. His wisdom is infinite, His strength is perfect, and His love for His children is unbreakable. When we look to Him as our Rock and Refuge, we are worshiping Him and giving Him glory.

4. True Worship Delights in God's Forgiveness (Psalm 32)

We cannot talk about wholehearted worship without addressing the confession of, repentance from, and cleansing of sin. After all, only the person whose sin has been completely dealt with can enjoy unhindered fellowship with God. In Psalm 32, David teaches us how to worship by delighting in the forgiveness of sin.

David's sin with Bathsheba will be discussed at length in chapter 7, so we won't belabor it here. Suffice it to say, David was guilty of adultery, murder, and a scandalous cover-up (2 Samuel 11). But after being confronted by the prophet Nathan, David confessed his sin and repented. When he did, he finally experienced freedom from the guilt and heartache he had been bottling up inside.

Psalm 32 is David's joy-filled response to being forgiven by God and restored to fellowship with Him. Overwhelmed by God's mercy, David exclaimed, "How blessed is he whose transgression is forgiven, whose sin is covered!" (verse 1). One translation says, "How *happy* is the one whose transgression is forgiven" (HCSB). David had finally repented. His sin was out in the open. God had lifted his burden and the result was pure, exhilarating happiness! Although his sin would result in serious consequences for both himself and his family, he was overjoyed nonetheless. How could that be?

David understood the gravity of his sin before God, describing it as a "transgression" (verse 1). He had violated God's law and knew the implications. Capital offenses had been committed. The guilt of his unconfessed sin weighed so heavily on his soul that it made him physically sick (verses 3-4). He could not eat, and his body "wasted away."

But after he confessed his sin, he was happy. Why? Again, the answer is found in the fact that David's focus was on God, and not on himself. His joy was rooted in the knowledge not of his sin and shame, but of the Lord's gracious character. God had forgiven and restored David, and he understood the significance of his pardon. His sins were covered. His burden was gone. Once again he could experience the joy and satisfaction of fellowship with God. He could not help but respond with words of total bliss!

As David demonstrates in Psalm 32, we worship God when we confess our sin. Do you delight in God's forgiveness? Is your heart happy in Him? The reality is that you will never know the nearness of God until you have dealt with your sin. You cannot know the happiness of having your sins covered unless you begin to understand the gravity of your transgressions before God—and then remember who you are because of Christ! Humble yourself, confess your sin, and find forgiveness. Then God will be glorified. He will draw near to you, and your heart will be filled with the joy of worship.

5. *True Worship Centers on the Cross (Psalm 22)*

All of Scripture points to Christ, and the Psalms are no exception. To remember who we are in Christ, we must consider the cross. For the believer, true wholehearted worship begins and ends there. Psalm 22 brings us face to face with the spiritual, emotional, and physical suffering of our Savior on the cross. Charles Spurgeon said of this psalm, "We should read reverently, putting off our shoes from off our feet, as Moses did at the burning bush, for if there be holy ground anywhere in Scripture it is in this Psalm."[4]

David, writing under the inspiration of the Holy Spirit (Acts 2:30), is given prophetic insight into the cross centuries before the Messiah came. Though the psalm may reflect some of David's trials, it clearly goes far beyond his own life and circumstances. It finds full meaning only in Jesus Christ. The New Testament confirms this for us, quoting from Psalm 22 seven times, all in reference to the Savior.

In Matthew 27:46, Jesus Himself quoted from this psalm when He cried out from the cross, "My God, my God, why have You forsaken Me?" (verse 1). We see expressions of suffering all throughout the psalms, but none deeper than this. This is different. It is suffering so deep we cannot fully comprehend it. Psalm 22:1-2 give us a glimpse into the anguish experienced by the Son of God as He bore our sins on the cross and as His Father turned His face away from Him. In that moment, God "made Him who knew no sin to be sin on our behalf" (2 Corinthians 5:21). Therein lies the great doctrine of substitution. The Father punished the Son for our sins so that He might clothe us in Christ's righteousness. And in Psalm 22, a thousand years before that unfathomable transaction took place, we see the heart of the gospel.

And yet even in the midst of suffering there is worship. The psalm continues, "Yet You are holy, O You who are enthroned upon the praises of Israel. In You our fathers trusted; they trusted and You delivered them. To You they cried out and were delivered; in You they trusted and were not disappointed" (verses 3-5). Even at the moment of greatest suffering, Christ's confidence in the Father was unshaken. There was no second-guessing or sinful response. He found assurance in remembering and affirming the Father's faithful character.

In Psalm 22:6-11, David further described the emotional suffering of the cross. "I am a worm and not a man, a reproach of men and despised by the people" (verse 6). Oh, what a thought! Because of our sin, the Son of God was brought so low that He could be compared to the most insignificant and lowly of all creation—*a worm.* He was despised. He was mocked. He was scorned. But all the while, He was sinless.

David continued by depicting the physical suffering of Christ. Psalm 22:12-21 brings us to the very foot of the cross, where Jesus died for you and me. He was weak. His strength was gone (verses 14-15). The weight of His body hung from the torn flesh of His pierced hands and feet (verse 16). His bones were slowly pulled out of joint (verse 14) as the excruciating agonies of crucifixion took their toll. He was beaten. He was broken. And still, He remained sinless.

That was the death that you and I deserved. Because of our sin, we should have been subject to that kind of humiliation, suffering, and separation from God. But there is victory in the cross. Jesus is our substitute! Because of what He accomplished in His death and resurrection, we will never know the unspeakable despair of separation from God. That is the gospel in all of its glorious mystery. Christ endured what He did not deserve so that we might enjoy what we do not deserve. Charles Wesley said it this way: "Amazing love! How can it be, that Thou my God shouldst die for me?"[5]

Verses 22-31 depict what was accomplished through the cross. Sinners were forgiven and are able to enjoy eternal fellowship with God. As David explained, "Those who seek Him will praise the LORD. Let your heart live forever!" (verse 26). The psalm even anticipates the church, as worshippers come both from Israel (verse 23) and the ends of the earth (verse 27). Those who have been bought by His blood will tell, from generation to generation, of what He has accomplished (verses 30-31).

All that the psalmist has taught us in our study of true worship is displayed completely, with sinless perfection, in Jesus Christ. The deepest suffering that our Savior endured was not the great physical and emotional pain He experienced on the cross. It was the separation from fellowship with His Father. And yet, even from the cross, Jesus remained confident in His Father's character and faithfulness. He found satisfaction in God alone. And He delighted in the forgiveness of our sin—His innocent blood was poured out for that very purpose (Matthew 26:28).

A CALL TO WHOLEHEARTED WORSHIP

Godly men love to worship. Resolve in your soul to follow the example of the psalmist. Humble yourself, acknowledge your need for God, and confess your sin. Reflect on His character and remember His faithfulness. Treasure His Word and delight in it. Glory in the gospel of Jesus Christ and saturate your soul in the excellent truths of our sovereign Lord.

Find your satisfaction in Him—seek to be consumed with the knowledge of God in Christ and—music or no music—your heart will overflow in praise, thanksgiving, and wholehearted worship!

6

Real Men Flee Temptation
Lessons from the Life of Timothy

ANDREW GUTIERREZ

eal men do *what?*

Growing up as a child who watched and played sports in Northern California, I can vividly remember a slogan the Oakland Raiders once used to heighten fan participation: "Real Men Wear Black." Certainly this was a catchy promotional tool for a professional football team. But more than that, it told men that if they were truly masculine they would wear a particular color of clothing that was anything but light or soft. Black is to be worn by men. Black is intimidating. Black says, "I'm dangerous. Look out." The slogan appeared everywhere, and even today, the image conveyed by the Raiders is that of being dangerous, proud, and a bit rebellious.

A simple slogan wouldn't normally be cause for great alarm. But what's troubling is the fact it represents a widespread cultural mindset. Masculinity, in our world, is often defined in terms of brute strength, brash independence, material wealth, ruthless power, or romantic charm. But the Bible has a different perspective on what it means to be a real man. Paul, instructing the men of Corinth toward true masculinity, wrote, "Be on the alert, stand firm in the faith, act like men, be strong" (1 Corinthians 16:13). True masculinity doesn't idolize sports, money, status, or the passing pleasures of this world. The lusts of the flesh come naturally to sinners, and any self-indulgent boy can consume himself with his own desires. But a real man does what is hard. He is a fighter, but not in the sense that the Raiders meant. Rather he fights for his Savior's glory, for his own sanctification, and for the spiritual good of those around him.

One chief way to do this is to flee temptation. Yes, that's right—real men run away. If sin is the great enemy of the Christian, then a man of God must be a skilled soldier in putting to death the sin that remains in his life. Puritan John Owen said it best: "Be killing sin, or it will be killing you."[1] Real men not only flee from sin, but from the temptation that precedes sin. For an excellent example of that principle, we need to look no further than the pages of the New Testament.

A YOUNG MAN NAMED TIMOTHY

Timothy had grown up in a God-fearing home—his mother and grandmother faithfully taught him the Scriptures. We are first introduced to Timothy in the book of Acts. There we are told, "Paul... came to Derbe and to Lystra. And a disciple was there, named Timothy, the son of a Jewish woman who was a believer, but his father was a Greek, and he was well spoken of by the brethren who were in Lystra and Iconium" (Acts 16:1-2). This young man would quickly become one of Paul's dearest companions and most trusted colaborers. He had a good reputation in his hometown, but God had bigger plans for Timothy and called him to become one of the chief workers in proclaiming the gospel message throughout the Gentile world.

But living the Christian life was not always easy for Timothy, even after he became a pastor in Ephesus. As we learn from Paul's letters to Timothy, the young man was engaged in a daily spiritual battle—fighting hard to shepherd his own soul and the souls of those under his care. The apostle exhorted his young disciple to suffer for Christ, guard the truth, and diligently handle the Scriptures. While young Timothy was mature beyond his years, as a Christian man he understood what it meant to be in a constant war against sin and temptation.

TIMOTHY'S EXAMPLE IN RESISTING TEMPTATION

In this chapter, using Timothy as our model, we will examine four key elements to resisting temptation in a way that honors the Lord.

1. *Request Help from God*

Have you ever felt like your battle against sin was impossible to win? Perhaps you've thought, *I want to flee from temptation, but at times it seems like I just can't.* If so, you are not alone. The apostle Paul essentially said that very thing in Romans 7. He wrote, "I have the desire to do what is right, but not the ability to carry it out. For I do not do the good I want, but the evil I do not want is what I keep on doing" (verses 18-19 ESV). Even Paul understood the daily battle between his spirit and his flesh. But the apostle's words did not end in despair. In the end, he looked to God for help and final victory. In triumph, he declared, "Who will set me free from the body of this death? Thanks be to God through Jesus Christ our Lord!... Therefore there is now no condemnation for those who are in Christ Jesus. For the law of the Spirit of life in Christ Jesus has set you free from the law of sin and of death" (Romans 7:24–8:2).

The disciples experienced a similar struggle—their mind telling them to do one thing but their flesh wanting another. On the night Jesus was betrayed, while in the Garden of Gethsemane, He asked His disciples to pray for Him as He prepared for the cross. They loved Him dearly and would have done anything they could to defend Him. But in that moment, they couldn't even keep their eyes open long enough to stay on the lookout. What was Jesus' response? "Keep watching and praying that you may not enter into temptation; the spirit is willing, but the flesh is weak" (Matthew 26:41). Because He recognized the frailty of the human condition, Jesus commanded His disciples (and by extension, all believers) to prayerfully depend on God's strength for victory over temptation.

In Hebrews 4, some of the most encouraging words in all of Scripture are written for those struggling to flee temptation. Speaking of Christ, the author of Hebrews explained, "We do not have a high priest who cannot sympathize with our weaknesses, but One who has been tempted in all things as we are, yet without sin" (verse 15). How comforting it is to know that Christ Himself understands what it is like to endure temptation and gain victory over it! Being wholly God, He could never sin. Yet being wholly man, He felt the full weight of temptation pressing against Him. When Satan tempted Him in the wilderness, Jesus had gone without food for 40 days. He was famished and physically weak. Yet even in that depleted condition, He prevailed over the devil's false promises. His victory over temptation would continue all the way to the cross, where He finally conquered sin once for all.

Having endured the most severe temptations imaginable, Jesus is sympathetic to the ways in which we are weak at the moment of testing. Our right response, when facing temptation, is to turn to Him for help. The author of Hebrews made this very point: "Therefore let us draw near with confidence to the throne of grace, so that we may receive mercy and find grace to help in time of need" (verse 16). If we are to find victory over temptation, we must depend on the Lord for strength and grace.

Timothy understood the need to ask God for help in the fight against temptation. As one of Paul's missionary companions, he had seen his mentor kneel in prayer many times. On one occasion Paul requested prayer from the Ephesians, just in case he might be tempted by cowardice (Ephesians 6:19-20). Timothy too was susceptible to the sin of cowardice (2 Timothy 1:7-8). So Paul instructed him to pray—specifically for those whom he might be tempted to fear, such as government officials (1 Timothy 2:1-8). As persecution against the church mounted, Timothy surely remembered Paul's words in Philippians 4:6: "Be anxious for nothing, but in everything by prayer and supplication with thanksgiving let your requests be made known to God." Having been well taught by his mentor, Timothy knew that the only right way to respond to his fears was to pray.

Even at the end of Paul's life, when everyone had deserted him, the apostle continued to encourage Timothy with the fact that "the Lord stood with [him] and strengthened [him]" (2 Timothy 4:17). The message for Timothy was clear: No matter what hardships he faced, he could depend on Christ. That lesson proved invaluable to the young pastor. When Timothy was later sent to prison, he resisted his fears and remained faithful to the Lord (cf. Hebrews 13:23).

2. Remember the Gospel

Paul, in his letters to Timothy, repeatedly reminded his young disciple of the truth of the gospel. He called him to remember "that Christ Jesus came into the world to save sinners" (1 Timothy 1:15); that He "gave Himself as a ransom for all" (2:6); and that He "testified the good confession before Pontius Pilate" (6:13). And he urged Timothy to "join with [him] in suffering for the gospel according to the power of God, who has saved us and called us with a holy calling, not according to our works, but according to His own purpose and grace which was granted us in Christ Jesus from all eternity" (2 Timothy 1:8-9). Paul never forgot that he was a sinner saved by grace (cf. 1 Timothy 1:15). And that reality motivated him toward faithfulness (cf. Ephesians 3:8).

It should motivate us as well. God sent His Son from heaven to earth in order to save those who had rebelled against Him. Not only has He rescued us from sin, but He calls us His children. Not only that, He promises to give us eternal rewards. That lavish treatment is just a taste of how abundantly God has showered the believer with undeserved blessings.

But when we yield to temptation, we act as though the passing pleasures of sin are more desirable than the infinite riches God has given us through Jesus Christ. In that moment, we operate like practical atheists—as though God did not exist or the gospel did not matter. It has been said that "Satan does not here fill us with hatred of God, but with forgetfulness of God." Very often that is true.

Reading the Word, singing praise choruses, memorizing verses, and talking to others about the gospel are all practical ways to safeguard the mind against temptation. Being repeatedly reminded of Christ's death and resurrection and the wonder of His substitutionary sacrifice is an effective antidote to sin. Conversely, those who forget the gospel or treat it lightly will find victory over temptation to be practically impossible.

That is why Paul emphasized the gospel in his letters to Timothy. He also warned his young disciple about those who had rejected that truth. There were those who "straying from these things, [had] turned aside to fruitless discussion" (1 Timothy 1:6). Others had "rejected [the gospel] and suffered shipwreck in regard to their faith" (verse 19). Looking ahead to the future, Paul warned that "in later times some will fall away from the faith, paying attention to deceitful spirits and doctrines of demons, by means of the hypocrisy of liars seared in their own conscience as with a branding iron" (4:1-2).

Paul then explicitly told Timothy, "If anyone advocates a different doctrine and does not agree with sound words, those of our Lord Jesus Christ, and with the doctrine conforming to godliness, he is conceited and understands nothing" (6:3-4). Such false teachers "oppose the truth [and are] men of depraved mind, rejected in regard to the faith" (2 Timothy 3:8). Soon they would be judged by God (verse 9). But as for Timothy, he was to "guard what [had] been entrusted to [him]" (1 Timothy 6:20), and "remember Jesus Christ, risen from the dead, descendant of David, according to [the true] gospel" (2 Timothy 2:8). If Timothy hoped to avoid temptation, especially the sin of apostasy, he desperately needed to remember the gospel of grace.

3. Run with the Godly

Imagine tuning in to watch a football game and hearing the star running back, during the pregame interview, say he would prefer for his linemen to stay on the sidelines. He is confident he doesn't need their help. Instead, he wants to make the plays against the opposing team all by himself. He says all he needs is someone to snap him the ball.

Obviously, that kind of thinking would be ludicrous. Without any blockers, the overconfident running back would get pummeled. Yet how often do we behave similarly in our fight against sin? We know the Bible commands us to "flee from youthful lusts" (2 Timothy 2:22), but we also need to remember that there is more to that command. Paul told Timothy, "Now flee from youthful lusts *and pursue righteousness, faith, love and peace, with those who call on the Lord from a pure heart*" (emphasis added). The fight against temptation is more than just running away from sin. As Paul explained to Timothy, it includes running *toward* spiritual fruit ("righteousness, faith, love and peace"). And it also involves running *with* other mature Christians ("with those who call on the Lord from a pure heart").

In football, the running back does not merely run away from the defenders who are trying to tackle him. He also runs toward a goal—a first-down marker, and ultimately, the end zone. He pursues that objective so that he can score points and achieve victory. Similarly, the Christian should pursue righteousness, faith, love, and peace as he flees from sin. The Puritan pastor Matthew Henry said it this way:

> The exciting of our graces will be the extinguishing of
> our corruptions; the more we follow that which is good

> the faster and the further we shall flee from that which
> is evil. Righteousness, and faith, and love, will be excel-
> lent antidotes against youthful lusts. Holy love will cure
> impure lust.[2]

Instead of focusing solely on what to avoid, Christian men are called to pursue the type of character they desire, a character that runs contrary to youthful lusts (and is consistent with the fruit of the Spirit). Doing this requires personal effort, as Paul told Timothy in 1 Timothy 4:7: "Discipline yourself for the purpose of godliness." But it also necessitates the mutual support of other believers. By joining with "those who call on the Lord with a pure heart," believers can find the encouragement and accountability they need to stave off temptation.

Conversely, Paul warned Timothy to stay away from harmful spiritual influences—people who would tempt him to sin. The apostle described those magnets of immorality with these words: "For men will be lovers of self, lovers of money, boastful, arrogant, revilers, disobedient to parents, ungrateful, unholy, unloving, irreconcilable, malicious gossips, without self-control, brutal, haters of good, treacherous, reckless, conceited, lovers of pleasure rather than lovers of God, holding to a form of godliness, although they have denied its power" (2 Timothy 3:2-5). Notice how Paul instructs Timothy to respond to these types of people: "Avoid such men as these" (2 Timothy 3:5).

That is a command that we must obey if we are serious about our ability to flee temptation. As the saying goes, bad company corrupts good morals. We must surround ourselves with those who are living righteous lives. By running the race with them, we will be spurred on toward greater holiness.

4. Resist the Temptation

The final way we must combat temptation is to simply resist. We must flee and escape. Timothy knew the importance of running away. Paul exhorted Timothy toward escaping temptation in each of his two letters to him. We have already looked at what 2 Timothy 2:22 says about fleeing youthful lusts. A similar admonition is found in 1 Timothy 6:11. After warning about the dangers of loving money, Paul wrote, "Flee from these things, you man of God, and pursue righteousness, godliness, faith, love, and perseverance and gentleness." In the next verse Paul then exhorted Timothy, "Fight the good fight of faith; take hold of the eternal life to which you were called, and you made the good confession in the presence of many witnesses" (verse 12).

When temptation came knocking, Timothy was to *flee* from sin and *fight* for faithfulness. As a pastor, he would have instructed other believers to do the same. Some years earlier, when Paul had sent Timothy to help the church in Corinth, the apostle told the Corinthians, "For this reason I have sent to you Timothy, who is my beloved and faithful child in the Lord, and he will remind you of my ways which are in Christ, just as I teach everywhere in every church" (1 Corinthians 4:17). One of the things Paul taught the Corinthians, which Timothy would have reiterated to them, was instruction for combating sexual sin. In his first epistle to the Corinthians the apostle wrote, "Flee immorality. Every other sin that a man commits is outside the body, but the immoral man sins against his own body" (1 Corinthians 6:18). The response to sexual temptation, as with all sin, starts with running as far away from it as is possible.

At this point some might protest and say, "I've tried to flee, but it's too hard!" But what would Paul say in response? He told the Corinthians, "No temptation has overtaken you but such as is common to man; and God is faithful, who will not allow you to be tempted beyond what you are able, but with the temptation will provide the way of escape also, so that you will be able to endure it" (1 Corinthians 10:13). No temptation is greater than God's power; and He has promised that, for those who rest in His strength no temptation is ever irresistible. When we stop making excuses and start walking in faith-filled obedience we are assured the victory through Christ.

A CROWN FOR THE WINNER

In the first century AD, crowns were awarded to victorious military leaders, champion athletes, and dignitaries. In Paul's farewell to his beloved disciple he wrote of receiving such a reward from Jesus Christ. Think of the impact that thought must have had on Timothy. How encouraging would it be for him to hear his mentor's final words to him, which conveyed confidence and joy in Jesus Christ? Paul's hope, as expressed in 2 Timothy 4:7-8, reminded his protégé of the reason that he was fighting as a soldier and striving like an athlete. In spite of being in prison about to die, the apostle exulted, "I have fought the good fight, I have finished the course, I have kept the faith; in the future there is laid up for me the crown of righteousness, which the Lord, the righteous Judge, will award to me on that day; and not only to me, but also to all who have loved His appearing." No matter what the struggles looked like for Timothy, he could overcome temptation because of the hope he had in Christ.

History tells us that Timothy died while trying to stop people from engaging in idolatry at a pagan feast. As he proclaimed the true gospel, he was severely beaten by the angry crowd and died two days later. Timothy gave up his life so that Christ would be glorified. He exhibited faithfulness and courage to the end.

As we flee from sin and pursue holiness in our own lives, let's follow the example of Timothy. By relying on God's strength, reminding ourselves of the gospel, and running away from sin and toward righteousness, we too can experience a life of spiritual victory. The road will not always be easy, but our faithfulness will be well-rewarded. One day, we will stand before Christ. Then sin and temptation will be no more. As we look forward to that day, we can rejoice with Paul in knowing that "the Lord will rescue [us] from every evil deed, and will bring [us] safely into His heavenly kingdom; to Him be the glory forever and ever. Amen" (2 Timothy 4:18).

Real Men Repent from Sin

Lessons from the Life of David

MARK ZHAKEVICH

Repentance, or turning from sin, is an essential component of the Christian life. It begins at the moment of salvation (Luke 24:47) and continues as we walk with Christ (1 John 1:9). Having turned to follow Him, we must continually put off the sins that so easily entangle us (Hebrews 12:1). As the nineteenth-century preacher Charles Spurgeon so aptly put it, "A Christian must never leave off repenting, for I fear he never leaves off sinning."[1] Though repentance is essential to our spiritual intimacy with God, it is not easily solicited from the heart. Repentance demands brokenness, humility, hatred of sin, and a genuine desire to change. It requires the concession that I was wrong and that I need forgiveness and restoration. Sometimes that admission is as difficult for us as it was for David, the man whose life we will consider in this chapter.

A MAN AFTER GOD'S OWN HEART

David is frequently hailed as a model of repentance. Though he was a man after God's own heart (1 Samuel 13:14), his life was certainly not free from sin. One tragic choice in particular resulted in adultery, murder, and a lengthy cover-up. Those were not small sins! Yet repentance is most intense where sin is greatest, and it is at this low point in David's life that we learn a number of important lessons.

With the exception of David's epic battle against Goliath, David's love affair with Bathsheba is probably the most well-known account of his life. The tragic episode began when David's army captain, Joab, led Israel's military on a campaign against the Ammonites while David stayed home in Jerusalem (2 Samuel 11). Late one afternoon, while taking a walk on the roof of his palace, David looked down and saw a woman bathing. Rather than resisting temptation and looking the other way, he allowed the lust of his eyes to incite the lust of his flesh. After some inquiry, he discovered that the woman was Bathsheba, "daughter of one of David's best fighters, the granddaughter of his most trusted counselor and the wife of one of his inner circle of honored soldiers."[1] Her pedigree should have stifled his interest, but instead he invited her to his palace. His adultery was followed by an unplanned pregnancy, a devious conspiracy, and a shameful murder.

For nine months David thought his cover-up had been successful. The more time that went by, the more it looked like he had gotten away with his sin. Repentance was a distant thought. As one author explained, "By delay of repentance, sin strengthens, and the heart hardens. The longer ice freezes, the harder it is to be broken."[2] Such was certainly true of David. Perhaps he thought he had concealed his actions well enough that no one knew what had really happened. Or perhaps he didn't care if others knew. After all, he was the king, and who would dare criticize him? But God knew what had happened. He would not let David's sin slip by silently.

The Lord sent His prophet Nathan to rebuke David. And in that moment, David's heart was pierced. All his schemes came crashing down as nine months of guilt and grief burst forth. In response to

Nathan's confrontation, David wrote some of the most precious and instructive words concerning repentance in all of Scripture. His tear-filled prayer, recorded in Psalm 51, reveals to us seven elements of genuine repentance. These elements characterize a right response to sin and exemplify the truth that real men repent.

1. The Repentant Heart Appeals to God's Grace

David's confession began with an appeal to the sole source of forgiveness—God Himself. David was no longer covering up his sin. He had run out of excuses. He had finally come before the Lord, broken, exhausted, and desperate. As he began his confession in verse 1, he took refuge not in himself but in the merciful character of God. By asking the Lord to "be gracious," David acknowledged both his own unworthiness and God's all-sufficient goodness. By appealing to the Lord's "lovingkindness," David reminded Him of His covenant love toward Abraham, Isaac, Jacob, and even David himself. By invoking "the greatness of [God's] compassion," David found refuge in the Lord's tenderness toward His people.

Repeatedly and completely, David threw himself at the mercy of God. He knew his own unworthiness. If he was to find forgiveness, he must look to the inexhaustible riches of God's gracious character. Perhaps he remembered God's self-description in Exodus 34: "The Lord, the Lord God, compassionate and gracious, slow to anger, and abounding in lovingkindness and truth" (verse 6). Every prayer of repentance must begin there—with a recognition of our total dependence on God's grace. For the New Testament believer, that grace is abundantly available in Jesus Christ, through whom we have received grace upon grace (John 1:16).

Jesus solidified the importance of resting in God's grace by telling a story about a Pharisee and a tax collector (Luke 18:9-14). While the former proudly paraded his self-righteous achievements, the latter humbly begged God for mercy. One trusted in his own merit to obtain God's favor, the other was "unwilling to lift up his eyes to heaven, but was beating his breast, saying, 'God, be merciful to me, the sinner!'" (Luke 18:13). Jesus affirmed that only the tax collector went home forgiven and justified. All true repentance begins with a heartfelt appeal to God's grace; otherwise, the process is cut short from the start.

2. *The Repentant Heart Admits Its Sin*

After appealing to God's grace, David admitted his sin (verses 2-3). He finally acknowledged the grievous nature of his actions. His nine-month cover-up was over (cf. 2 Samuel 11:27; 12:1). It was time to stop lying to himself, to others, and to God about what he had done. As Andrew Murray observed, "Man is by nature so entirely under the power of sin that he can hide it from himself even when he has committed it. This is one of the most dangerous manifestations of sin. It blinds the heart…It is the work of the Spirit of the grace of God to make the soul acknowledge sin."[3] In this case, God graciously sent His prophet to confront David's sin and bring conviction to his heart. The result was genuine confession, including an admission of wrongdoing, an agreement with God as to the seriousness of the offense, a willingness to accept the consequences, and a sincere desire to change.

Notably, David did not shift the blame. He took full responsibility. Throughout the psalm, he repeatedly affirmed that it was *his* wrongdoing; thus, he wrote of "*my* transgressions" (verse 1), "*my* iniquity" (verse 2), "*my* sin" (verse 2), "*my* transgressions" (verse 3), "*my* sin" (verse 3), and so on. David did not accuse Bathsheba of being a temptress. He did not complain about the proximity of her husband's house to his palace (such that he could see her bathing). He did not blame his army captain, Joab, for helping him carry out the plot against Uriah. Instead, he openly admitted what James wrote in the New Testament—that "each one is tempted when he is carried away and enticed by his *own* lust. Then when lust has conceived, it gives birth to sin" (James 1:14-15, emphasis added). David's sin was his own, and he acknowledged that fact to God. Genuine confession does not attempt to justify the wrongdoing. It does not blame Satan or other people. Rather, it takes responsibility for its actions by making a specific admission of sin. Then it rests in the grace and mercy of God for forgiveness and cleansing.

3. The Repentant Heart Asks for Forgiveness

In Psalm 32, a parallel passage to Psalm 51, David spoke of the joy that comes from seeking and receiving God's forgiveness. He wrote, "How blessed is he whose transgression is forgiven, whose sin is covered!...I acknowledged my sin to You, and my iniquity I did not hide; I said, 'I will confess my transgressions to the Lord'; and You forgave the guilt of my sin" (verses 1,5). The guilt that had burdened him those many months was finally lifted (cf. verses 3-4). Having been forgiven, he could "shout for joy" along with all "who are upright in heart" (verse 11).

As David had come to understand, sincere repentance seeks forgiveness. In Psalm 51, he used eight different phrases to make the singular request, "God, please forgive me." In verse 1, he said, "Blot out my transgressions"; in verse 2, "Wash me from my iniquity," and "Cleanse me from my sin." In verse 7, he pleaded, "Purify me with hyssop," and "Wash me." In verse 9, he begged God, "Hide your face from my sins," and "Blot out all my iniquities." And in verse 14, he made one final appeal: "Deliver me from blood-guiltiness, O God, the God of my salvation." David stood condemned before the law. He had murdered, committed adultery, coveted, and borne false witness by trying to cover everything up. He had acted upon the lust in his heart and ended up with blood on his hands. No earthly priest could absolve him from those sins. So David entreated God for mercy.

David knew that the stain of sin had made him dirty. So he begged God to wipe off (or blot out) his sin as one would wipe away dirt. He also understood that the disease of sin, like a spiritual

form of leprosy, had left him contaminated. Thus, he needed to
be cleansed (verse 2) and washed with hyssop (verse 7), an agent
used for the ceremonial cleansing of lepers (Leviticus 14:6-7). In
the same way that lepers were outcasts in ancient Israel, so David's
sin had made him an outcast from the presence of God. As a result,
he longed for God to forgive him and restore to him the joy of salvation (verse 12).

David's sin was strategically planned, but so was his confession.
He sought complete and thorough cleansing so that no residue of
sin would remain (cf. Psalm 103:12). That same desire should characterize our repentance as we ask the Lord for daily cleansing from
the sins we commit. Godly men don't shift blame or make excuses.
Instead, they regularly confess their sins and seek forgiveness (cf.
1 John 1:9).

4. The Repentant Heart Acknowledges the Offended Party

In Psalm 51:4, David opened with a shocking statement. Speaking to God, he wrote, "Against You, You only, I have sinned." But
what about Bathsheba? What about Uriah? What about their
extended families? What about the nation David was supposed to
be leading? The impact of David's sin affected the lives of countless
people. Yet he rightly understood that his actions were ultimately
an offense to the Lord.

Every sin, at its core, is an act of rebellion against God. Sin disre-
gards His law, attempts to usurp His authority, and flies in the face
of His holy character. Not only that, every sin is performed in God's
presence (Proverbs 15:3). When we sin, we do so in full view of our
holy Creator. Charles Spurgeon said that David "felt that his sin was
committed in all its filthiness while Jehovah himself looked on."[4]
In addition to seeing our actions, God knows our wicked thoughts,
motives, and attitudes too. Nothing is hidden from His omniscient
sight (Hebrews 4:13).

Genuine repentance recognizes that sin is utterly loathsome

to God. He hates it. He must punish it. One day, He will utterly destroy it. When we view our sin from His perspective, we see how wretched and vile it truly is. Too often, Christians today lower their standard of holiness, allowing it to reflect the growing worldliness of our society. The result is a lax attitude toward sanctification and a harmful tolerance toward sin, even in the church. But we must not allow the culture around us to dictate our thinking. Our standard of holiness is God Himself (1 Peter 1:16). When our actions violate His perfect character, we must come to Him with a heart full of humility and contrition (Isaiah 66:2).

5. *The Repentant Heart Aspires for Full Restoration with God*

As believers, we were fully forgiven at the moment of salvation, having been declared righteous before God based on the finished work of Christ. The wondrous truth of justification means that we have been pardoned for our transgressions. Our debts have all been paid, and the Judge of the Universe has officially declared us "Not guilty." Through the cross, our sins have been covered once for all.

But even though we've been declared righteous, the reality is that we don't always live righteously. We still sin in this life (1 John 1:8,10), and when we do, our relationship with God is hindered. We have been adopted into His family, and that adoption is permanent. God will never disown us (cf. John 10:28-29; Romans 8:38-39). Yet our sin still puts a strain on the fellowship we enjoy with our heavenly Father. And if we don't repent, we can expect Him to chastise us just as an earthly father disciplines the children whom he loves (Hebrews 12:3-11).

Every believer is devastated by sin because sin creates a chasm in one's relationship with the most precious Person in the universe. That was David's experience, and his cry for restoration is understandable. The man after God's own heart yearned for the nearness with God he had once enjoyed.

In Psalm 32:3-4, David said he was wasting away and groaning all day long due to the weight of his sin. According to Psalm 38:2, it was as if God's hand was pressing down on him and arrows were piercing him. He was crushed, agitated, wounded, and depressed—all due to his sin! It is no wonder David asked God to restore the bones which He had broken and to fill him with joy and gladness (Psalm 51:8).

The repentant sinner longs for the damaged relationship with God to be made right. His deep desire is to see his fellowship with God restored. Through confession, the wall of sin is removed and communion with God becomes intimate once again. And no matter how many steps away from God have been taken, the glorious truth is that it's only one step back. Repentance brings restoration. And restoration with God brings His supernatural peace and joy.

6. The Repentant Heart Announces the Gospel of Forgiveness

Over and over in Scripture, the reception of forgiveness is immediately followed by evangelistic zeal. The Samaritan woman told her entire village about the One who had exposed her sin and offered her living water (John 4:39). The demon-possessed man of the Gerasenes proclaimed his deliverance to those living across the Sea of Galilee (Mark 5:19-20). Immediately after Paul was converted and had regained his sight, "he began to proclaim Jesus in the synagogues" (Acts 9:20). He was so committed to evangelism that he begged people to be reconciled to God (2 Corinthians 5:20). The soul that is restored to God will proclaim its reconciliation. Where there once was shame and guilt there is now a joyful exuberance that must be shared.

Once David experienced this restoration, he was enthused to tell others about God's cleansing grace. He wrote, "Restore to me the joy of Your salvation…Then I will teach transgressors Your ways, and sinners will be converted to You" (Psalm 51:12-13). Commenting on those verses, J.J. Perowne observed that "with a conscience set free from guilt, with a heart renewed by the Spirit of God, and full of thankfulness for God's great mercy, he cannot keep silent, but will seek to turn other sinners to God."[5] After David was forgiven, he became eager to teach others about the mercies of God.

That same evangelistic zeal should characterize all who have experienced the amazing grace of God's forgiveness. Do our prayers include intercession for others, that they might likewise be forgiven? Do our conversations with unbelievers highlight the marvelous good news of reconciliation to God? Do our interactions with fellow believers remind them to give thanks for the forgiveness they have received and continue to enjoy daily? Are we willing to lovingly confront a brother in Christ who is living in sin, pleading with him to repent and be restored to his heavenly Father? The heartbeat of one who has been forgiven is such that he longs for others to share in the exhilarating happiness of being right with God.

7. The Repentant Heart Advances the Pleasure of God

Repentance centers on God's glory and culminates in the advancement of His fame. The forgiven sinner will "joyfully sing of [God's] righteousness" (Psalm 51:14) because his transgression has been forgiven and his sin covered (Psalm 32:1). He will proclaim alongside the prophet Micah, "Who is a God like You, who pardons iniquity...?" (Micah 7:18). The penitent prayer does not end in sadness because forgiveness brings peace and joy (Psalm 51:12). And the joy-filled believer gladly gives glory to the God of grace.

David promised to vocalize God's glory with words of praise. He wrote, "My tongue will joyfully sing of Your righteousness. O Lord, open my lips, that my mouth may declare Your praise" (verses 14-15). He then committed himself to following up his repentance with acceptable sacrifices to God (verse 19), which stemmed from a heart of brokenness and contrition (verse 17). Though we do not offer bulls and goats as sacrifices today, we are still commanded to render certain sacrifices to God. As the apostle Paul said in the book of Romans, "I urge you, brethren, by the mercies of God, to present your bodies a living and holy sacrifice, acceptable to God, which is your spiritual service of worship. And do not be conformed to this world, but be transformed by the renewing of your mind, so that you may prove what the will of God is, that which is good and acceptable and perfect" (12:1-2).

The author of Hebrews similarly instructed his readers, "Let us continually offer up a sacrifice of praise to God, that is, the fruit of lips that give thanks to His name" (Hebrews 13:15). Our offerings of worship today consist of words of praise and works of obedience. But God is pleased with such sacrifices only when they are offered from a truly penitent heart (cf. Psalm 51:16).

As believers, we have been saved so that we might be "to the praise of His glory" (Ephesians 1:12,14, see also 1:6). When we walk according to His will, we reflect His glory as living sacrifices—testifying to the truth of His sanctifying power. But even after we falter and fail, when we come to Him in humble repentance, He is quick to forgive and restore us. That too advances His glory, for it magnifies the inexhaustible riches of His grace and invokes within us a heart of thankful praise. Moreover, having been restored to unhindered fellowship with Him, we are ready to once again live a joy-filled Christian life through the power of His Spirit.

A GOD OF INEXHAUSTIBLE GRACE

Although delayed, David's repentance was genuine. What David tried to cover up, God uncovered. But once David openly confessed his sin, God covered it with grace. Humbled and convicted, David no longer ignored his sin. He did not try to justify it or shift the blame. Rather, he came to God with a broken and contrite heart. And God, true to His character, responded with grace, compassion, and forgiveness.

In this case, David's example does not magnify him. He had failed miserably. All he could do was admit his utter wrongdoing and plead for divine benevolence. But David's experience does magnify God's kindness and mercy—highlighting the fact that no sin is beyond the reach of His inexhaustible grace. Therein lies the hope for you, me, and every other sinner. Like David, we are all unworthy. But like David, we can each find forgiveness at the throne of grace. Only then, with our relationship to God restored, can we experience the joy of our salvation and the peace that passes all understanding.

Real Men Refuse to Compromise
Lessons from the Life of Daniel

KELLY WRIGHT

What would cause you to compromise? What would entice you to the point you'd be willing to forfeit your integrity and endanger your reputation? Could it be something as simple as candy? How about the promise of being made a prince and the thought of having your brother and sisters serve you as their king?

Those temptations proved too much for Edmund Pevensie. The promises of the White Witch included endless amounts of a treat called Turkish delight and a royal rule over Narnia. Such prospects sounded so good to Edmund that he was willing to deceive his siblings and endanger their lives to get what he wanted. But his willingness to compromise did not turn out well. The promises made by the White Witch were empty and false. Instead of enjoying Turkish delight, Edmund received a hunk of dry bread on an iron plate. And rather than being crowned prince of Narnia, he was subjected to the life of a slave. As the plot of C.S. Lewis's story *The Lion, the Witch, and the Wardrobe* continues to unfold, a harsh reality quickly surfaces: Edmund's foolish decision had devastating consequences for him and his family.

No one likes a compromiser—someone who would violate his stated principles and betray the trust of those who know him. Even in this fictitious story there is a sense of immediate disdain for Edmund on account of his willingness to sell out for something as petty as Turkish delight and as fantastic as the kingship of Narnia. The reader is left to wonder how the story might have gone if Edmund had possessed stronger convictions.

But before we point fingers at Edmund too quickly, we need to pause and consider our own hearts. *How often do we compromise?* We might not have betrayed our family for the sake of candy and a king's throne, but the reality is that every sin we commit is a form of spiritual capitulation. When we yield to the voice of temptation, living as though its false promises were true, we act just like Edmund did. How foolish we are when we choose the fleeting pleasures of sin over the eternally satisfying promises of God. Such is the folly and treachery of compromise.

CONSIDERING COMPROMISE

The opposite of compromise is *integrity*—the proven character that comes from consistent and courageous conviction. While a life of duplicity is natural to sinful man, a pattern of integrity is impossible apart from God's grace. Only those who have been saved from sin and are now being sanctified by the Holy Spirit can effectively resist temptation and live in patterns of uprightness. As believers grow in Christlikeness, their courage grows stronger and their convictions deepen—making them more ready to stand firm no matter what trials or temptations might come their way (1 Corinthians 10:13).

God has provided us with everything we need to walk in integrity. His work of regeneration has given us a new heart (2 Corinthians 5:17). His Spirit empowers us to obey (Romans 8:1-11). His spiritual armor enables us to resist the deceptive attacks of the evil one (Ephesians 6:10-18). And His divine power has granted us "everything pertaining to life and godliness" (2 Peter 1:3). When we walk according to that Word, applying its truth to every area of our lives, we can be confident that we are pleasing Him and walking with integrity.

As we immerse ourselves in the Scriptures, we also learn about the saints of old, men and women who received God's grace and responded in obedience. Though they were not perfect, their lives encourage us to follow in their footsteps, running the race of faith without compromise (see Hebrews 11). One such individual was the prophet Daniel.

We learn most about Daniel's life from the Old Testament book that bears his name. Written by him at the end of his life, the book's central theme is the sovereignty of God. For the Jewish exiles living in captivity in Babylon, its message offered great encouragement. The Babylonian army had conquered Jerusalem, destroyed the Temple, and taken the people captive to a faraway land. But in the book of Daniel God gives them hope, revealing a future in which His kingdom would be established on the earth. It is a future we still anticipate with eagerness and hope.

Daniel's own life reflected his confidence in God's sovereignty. Like every person, his character was a product of his theology. His view of God determined how he lived. As a result, he never wavered in his faith despite his surroundings. He worshiped the Lord and faithfully lived for Him, even when it was dangerous to do so. Daniel's circumstances were difficult, yet he did not betray his godly values. He was a man of conviction, courage, and consistency. As such, his life teaches us several vital lessons about integrity, underscoring the truth that no matter what the cost, real men refuse to compromise.

INTEGRITY IS NOT RESERVED FOR OLD MEN

It was six centuries before the Messiah would be born. Daniel, whose name means "God is my judge," was only a teenager. He and his friends found themselves hundreds of miles from home. As sons of the Jewish nobility, they had been selected by King Nebuchadnezzar—after his first invasion of Jerusalem—and taken by force to Babylon. There, they were taught the culture of the Chaldeans so that they could serve in Nebuchadnezzar's royal court.

From the moment they arrived in Babylon, Daniel and his friends were surrounded by idolatry. They were even given new names that reflected pagan deities. Daniel was renamed *Belteshazzar*, a name derived from Bel, the foremost deity in the Babylonian pantheon. Daniel's friends Hananiah, Mishael, and Azariah were also given new names: Shadrach, Meshach, and Abed-nego. With their very identities in question, the incentive to compromise must have been tempting. What better way could there be to succeed in Babylon than to fully embrace the culture there, including its religious practices?

But the resolve of these young men was undeterred. They would have nothing to do with pagan worship, refusing even to eat meat or drink wine that had been offered to idols. To enjoy such would have affirmed the false worship of Babylon and violated God's command not to eat anything unclean. So Daniel "made up his mind that he would not defile himself" (Daniel 1:8). Whatever the consequences might be, Daniel determined that he would not compromise.

According to Daniel 1:9, God granted Daniel favor with the commander of the officials, enabling him and his friends to dine on vegetables and water instead. To their supervisor's surprise, after a ten-day experiment, they were in better physical condition than everyone else. God had honored Daniel's faith. As the Lord told the high priest Eli many years earlier, "Those who honor Me I will honor" (1 Samuel 2:30). Daniel refused to compromise, and God blessed him for his integrity.

The amazing reality is that Daniel was only a teenager when this took place! He was young in years, growing in wisdom, and untested in life. Even so, his courageous stand in Babylon was undoubtedly not the first time he had decided to honor God. Scripture does not record Daniel's childhood in Jerusalem. But it is safe to assume that, from a very early age, Daniel had cultivated a resolute faith and steadfast love for the Lord.

As a young man Daniel knew it was more important to fear God than even King Nebuchadnezzar, the most powerful man in the world at the time. And the Lord continued to bless Daniel and his friends. At the end of their three-year training course, they were not only at the head of their class, they stood out from everyone else in the entire royal court. According to Daniel 1:20, "As for every matter of wisdom and understanding about which the king consulted them, he found them ten times better than all the magicians and conjurers who were in all his realm."

A second episode in Daniel's life reiterates the truth that integrity is not a matter of age, but one of courage and conviction. Daniel was likely still a teenager, freshly graduated from his Babylonian finishing school, when Nebuchadnezzar had a troubling dream.

Normally the king would explain his dream to his wise men and they would offer an interpretation. But this time, the king refused to tell anyone what he had dreamed. He demanded instead that his wise men tell him both what he had seen and what it meant. Not surprisingly, they were unable to do so. Nebuchadnezzar was furious at their response and decreed that on account of their failure all of his counselors should be killed. Suddenly, and through no doing of their own, Daniel and his friends found their lives in immediate danger. So how did Daniel respond?

He could have feared for his life, fled from the danger, or fought off the soldiers who came to arrest him. But such responses would have run contrary to everything he knew about God's sovereignty. Instead of growing anxious, Daniel responded in prayer (Daniel 2:14). He and his friends asked God to reveal the mystery of the king's dream to Daniel. And the Lord was pleased to grant their request.

When Daniel reported and explained Nebuchadnezzar's dream

to him, the king was so astonished that he "fell on his face" and said, "Surely your God is a God of gods and a Lord of kings and a revealer of mysteries, since you have been able to reveal this mystery" (verses 46-47). The king exalted God and also honored Daniel, promoting him to a position of authority over the entire province of Babylon.

Even as a teenager, Daniel's response to his circumstances revealed a heart of courage and conviction. He trusted in the sovereignty, wisdom, and grace of God. Having placed his confidence in the character of God, Daniel refused to compromise. His resolute faith made him a man of integrity.

Daniel's example teaches us that integrity is not reserved solely for men who have extensive life experience and gray hair. Integrity is expected of every follower of God. Every Christian man, no matter what his age, is called to flee from compromise and faithfully follow Christ. From the moment of salvation, believers are to "walk in a manner worthy of the calling with which [they] have been called" (Ephesians 4:1). Whether we are a young adult or an elderly saint, we are all held to the same standard of godly living.

INTEGRITY MUST BE CONSISTENT FOR IT TO COUNT

A man of integrity is a man of consistency. His character and conviction are the same in every situation. He is not defined by one good action, but by a lifetime of right choices.

That was certainly the case with Daniel. The young prophet's integrity did not end when he was a teenager. As he grew older, he remained faithful to the Lord—refusing to compromise no matter what the consequences.

The fourth chapter of Daniel records Nebuchadnezzar's pride, humiliation, and ultimate repentance. Once again, the king had a dream. But this time it was different—it predicted judgment on Nebuchadnezzar himself. Due to his pride, the king would be supernaturally subjected to seven years of madness and humiliation. According to verse 25, Nebuchadnezzar would be "driven away from mankind and [his] dwelling place [would] be with the beasts of the field, and [he would] be given grass to eat like cattle and be drenched with the dew of heaven; and seven periods of time [would] pass over [him], until [he came to] recognize that the Most High is ruler over the realm of mankind and bestows it on whomever He wishes."

When Nebuchadnezzar related the details of the dream to Daniel, Daniel was "appalled for a while as his thoughts alarmed him." He told the king, "If only the dream applied to those who hate you and its interpretation to your adversaries!" (verse 19). Faced with the uncomfortable prospect of telling Nebuchadnezzar some bad news, Daniel had to decide whether or not he would compromise his integrity. He could have lied about the dream's meaning and presented an interpretation that was favorable for the king. But he did not. Instead, because Daniel feared God more than the king, he faithfully explained to Nebuchadnezzar what God had revealed to him.

Of course, Daniel's response in that situation was not really a surprise, especially in light of what he had done earlier in his life. As a man of integrity, Daniel's character remained consistent. The conviction that marked him as a young man continued throughout his entire life. His character was such that his response to any given situation was predictable. And out of that consistency, a powerful reputation was forged.

Many years later, at about the age of 80, Daniel again proved his integrity before another Babylonian king, Belshazzar. The man of God was called to interpret mysterious words that a divine hand had written on a wall. One can imagine the 80-year-old prophet walking slowly but confidently into the banquet room where Belshazzar and his idolatrous friends had defiled gold vessels that had been taken from the Lord's Temple in Jerusalem.

The divinely inscribed message revealed Belshazzar's impending doom that very night. Again, Daniel might have been tempted to lie, portraying a positive interpretation so as to not incite Belshazzar's wrath. After all, the Babylonian kingdom was about to come to an end; perhaps it would be to Daniel's advantage to keep the bad news to himself. But, maintaining the integrity he had demonstrated all his life, he gave a correct interpretation of the words on the wall.

Daniel consistently feared the Lord rather than man. With his full confidence placed in God, he maintained his integrity despite any danger to his own life. After the fall of Belshazzar's kingdom to King Darius and the Medo-Persians, Darius appointed Daniel as one of three commissioners who had authority over 120 leaders of the kingdom. And once again, Daniel's integrity was put to the test.

Interoffice rivalry is nothing new. However, Daniel's colleagues took it to a whole new level—going so far as to devise a plan to have him killed. They plotted to set Daniel's obedience to God against his obedience to Darius (Daniel 6:4-5). Because they knew him to be a man of integrity, they knew exactly what he would do if he was forced to make a choice between obeying the Lord and obeying the king.

When the wicked leaders convinced the ego-hungry Darius to establish a new law requiring all his citizens to worship him alone for 30 days, the trap was set. Daniel's enemies knew he would not compromise. He would never worship Darius, nor would he ever stop worshiping the one true God. Though aware of the decree, Daniel maintained his practice of praying three times every day (Daniel 6:10). His enemies were happy to catch him in the act.

The infraction, which was punishable by death, sent Daniel to the lions' den. But just as God had honored Daniel's faithfulness to Him many years earlier, God honored Daniel again by protecting his life. The prophet's refusal to compromise was a testimony to Darius, who was overjoyed to find that Daniel was still alive after a full night in the lions' den. The leaders who devised Daniel's downfall were then thrown to the lions. And the king made a new decree: This time, the people in the kingdom were ordered to worship the one true God.

Daniel was consistent in his integrity. Whether the issue was his diet and avoiding food offered to idols, his willingness to interpret dreams accurately, or his faithful practice of worship, Daniel consistently lived for God. He did not fear court officials or kings more than he feared the Lord. As a result, he refused to compromise, even when the consequences were potentially deadly. What an example he is to us!

INTEGRITY IS THE FRUIT OF GODLY CHARACTER

Integrity doesn't just happen. It takes determination to cultivate integrity, which is the result of heartfelt conviction and godly character. Godliness must be cultivated in one's thoughts, words, and actions. And that requires diligent effort. The man who desires integrity must work hard to "discipline [himself] for the purpose of godliness" (1 Timothy 4:7).

Daniel's example teaches us that integrity is the fruit of godly character. Throughout his entire life, he pursued the Lord with all his heart. He worshiped God, lived by His Word, prayed often, and feared the Lord above all else. A God-centered focus characterized his life, and he acted accordingly.

The secret to Daniel's character was his understanding of God. He believed in God's power, faithfulness, and love. His knowledge of God's Word governed his life. Nothing could cause him to compromise his convictions because his integrity was grounded in his theology. He trusted wholeheartedly in the sovereignty of God, and enjoyed the Lord's blessing as a result. As one author has written:

> Daniel's experience is a tremendous illustration of God's sovereign blessing working together with man's complete commitment to the highest principles. Humanly speaking, Daniel's success depended on his own commitment. Divinely speaking, what happened to Daniel

was entirely under God's control. The complementary truths of sovereignty and commitment are inseparably linked and applicable in our lives as we seek to live uncompromisingly for Him. We can expect that our commitment to Daniel's extraordinary standards, which are really just God's ordinary standards, will be challenged and tested by the world (cf. John 16:33; James 1:2-3). But we can also be confident of positive results from those tests, just as Daniel was assured (cf. Job 23:10).[1]

Armed with a resolute faith in God, Daniel refused to compromise. As Christian men, we should not compromise either. Like Daniel, our lives ought to be governed by biblical principles and a right understanding of the Lord's perfect character. Our faith in Him should be the foundation for our unwavering convictions; and our love for Him the reason for our consistent obedience. The Lord paid an infinite price to save us, and we should take great joy in serving Him at any cost. Knowing that He will hold us accountable for the way we live, it is our delight to please Him in every decision. He is ever faithful and always true, so it our goal to honor Him by walking in integrity. After all, our reputation is not the only one at stake. We bear His name, and we never want to bring reproach upon our Savior.

Though Daniel was tested far from home by the most powerful kings of his day, he never compromised his convictions. He maintained a life of integrity before God because he feared the Lord more than he feared men. His character was marked by consistency and courage. And by the time he was an old man his reputation was so well established that even his enemies could count on it. What a testimony of integrity and godly discipline!

Believers today should be encouraged and challenged by Daniel's example. "Daniel didn't compromise, and neither should we. The scriptural principles upon which Daniel stood are just as real, practical, and reliable for us as they were for him."[2] To be men of integrity, we must be men of conviction, courage, and consistency. And by walking in a way that honors the Lord, we can rest in His sovereign control and enjoy His promised blessing on our lives.

9

Real Men Lead with Courage
Lessons from the Life of Nehemiah

JONATHAN ROURKE

No one kept statistics on quarterback sacks in the National Football League until 1982 because the event was never a game changer. That was before Lawrence Taylor. He was six foot four, 245 pounds, lightning fast, and on a mission to hurt whoever was holding the football. Quarterbacks in the league were so scared of number 56 that they would forget the snap count or call a timeout if they couldn't locate him on the defense. Sound extreme? Just ask quarterback Joe Theismann.

Leading an offense is difficult, especially when your opponent has a reputation for ending the career of people in your shoes. It takes courage, which is action in the face of fear. If you fail to act fast enough you might find yourself flat on your back, sacked by determined opponents or difficult circumstances. The Old Testament hero Nehemiah knew both, but he persevered and overcame adversity through his courage, determination, and zeal for God.

The account of Nehemiah teaches us that a godly leader needs to be willing to act on his convictions. It shows that part of developing the right character is being prepared to pay the price. You can do great things—even things beyond your natural ability—if you have great faith.

THE BASIS OF NEHEMIAH'S COURAGE

Nehemiah is a spiritual hero—a stellar example of integrity and virtue. Though there are many lessons we can learn from his life, in this chapter we will focus on his bold and brave leadership. Three dominant characteristics that were evident in his life help to explain the basis for his courage—namely, conviction, sacrifice, and faith.

Conviction: Courage Is Action-oriented

Stephen Siller had just finished his all-night shift at Brooklyn's Squad 1 firehouse. He was driving in his truck, on his way to play golf, when he heard the news about the attacks on the World Trade Center. Immediately he turned around and raced back. When he arrived at the Brooklyn Battery Tunnel, he was unable get through because all traffic had been halted. But that didn't stop him. He jumped out of his truck, grabbed 70 pounds of gear, and ran the three miles from the tunnel to Ground Zero. With no thought for his own life, the determined fireman courageously charged toward danger, sacrificing himself to help others. Siller never made it home that day, leaving behind a wife and five children. Yet his legacy of courage, along with the courage of his fellow firefighters, continues to inspire the multitudes who visit the 9/11 Memorial.

Stephen was motivated by a profound sense of duty and responsibility. It made him act immediately when others were paralyzed with fear and confusion. It was not an impulsive reaction, but a decisive one—based on years of training and an unwavering commitment to serve. In this way Stephen's courage reflects that of Nehemiah, a man who exhibited the same kind of resolute character 25 centuries earlier.

Nehemiah was a cupbearer for the most powerful man in the

world. He served the Persian emperor Artaxerxes in the capital city of Susa. One day the perceptive monarch noticed Nehemiah was sad and inquired as to the reason. When Nehemiah explained that his native Jerusalem lay in ruins, the king immediately asked him what he wanted to do about it. After a quick prayer, the bold servant asked for leave from his job, authority to travel through the kingdom without restriction, and sufficient building material to rebuild the gates and walls of the city. Surprisingly the king agreed.

This is the first example of Nehemiah's ability to act decisively. When the king asked Nehemiah a probing question, Nehemiah gave a prompt, specific, and conclusive answer. Men of courage are not fond of saying, "I don't know; let me check and get back to you." Nehemiah's response was decisive in the same way as Siller's was. His actions were prompted not simply by his circumstances, but by his convictions. God had been preparing Nehemiah throughout his entire life for the moment when the king would ask that critical question. And when it came, along with the opportunity to make something happen, Nehemiah did not hesitate to act.

Petitioning the king took great courage. But Nehemiah had already petitioned the King of kings long before he ever appealed to Artaxerxes. It is important to see that prayer was the real fuel for Nehemiah's courage. When Nehemiah had heard about the plight of the Jews in Jerusalem, he sat down, wept, and sought the Lord (Nehemiah 1:4). When he was questioned by the king, he quickly prayed first—and then he spoke (2:4). Later, while rebuilding the wall, Nehemiah faced insults and opposition, and asked God to turn back the reproach on the heads of his enemies (4:4). And when he was threatened, he both prayed for help and prepared to defend his people (4:9-14). Nehemiah's unwavering confidence in God, which was evidenced and empowered by his faithful prayer life, gave him courage even in the presence of those who opposed him.

Nehemiah was bold not only in response to his enemies, but also in his interactions with his peers. After the former cupbearer arrived in Jerusalem, he found the people facing a severe debt crisis. The Jewish nobility were charging them excessive interest on their loans, and the people appealed to Nehemiah for help. In a clear example of courageous leadership, Nehemiah said, "I took counsel with myself, and I brought charges against the nobles and the officials" (Nehemiah 5:7 ESV). A godly leader must sometimes make unilateral decisions based on what he knows is right.

For Nehemiah to do this wasn't easy. He needed the upper-class people in Jerusalem to support his administration, and he knew that the common people had legitimate concerns and needs. In this case, the lower classes had the moral high ground. It was wrong for brothers to take advantage of other brothers. The Jewish brotherhood was sacred, and the people were supposed to care for one another. So Nehemiah called a public assembly and appealed to the nobles from an ethical perspective. Doing so allowed them to retain their dignity by promising to do what was right in front of all the people. It also ensured that they would fulfill their promises, since they were now subject to public accountability. Nehemiah's strategy worked. He knew what needed to be done. He took counsel with himself, and acted.

Sacrifice: Courage Is Others-oriented

A second element of courageous leadership is personal sacrifice. The first time I read *The Chocolate Soldier, or, Heroism—the Lost Chord of Christianity* by C.T. Studd, I was mesmerized. I could not put it down because it began with such a powerful, blistering indictment that it left me wondering if I was missing the part of the book that led up to it. Studd was raised in a wealthy home, and in his prime he was considered one of the best cricket players in all of England. If anyone could have enjoyed an easy life, it was Studd. How simple it would have been to carry on as God had placed him, gracefully gliding through this short life on into eternity. But that was not how Studd would have it. After going to China as a missionary with Hudson Taylor, he divested himself of worldly comforts and embraced a sacrificial lifestyle for the sake of serving Christ.

He wrote,

> Every true Christian is a soldier of Christ, a hero 'par excellence'! Braver than the bravest, scorning the soft seduction of peace and her oft-repeated warning against hardship, disease, danger, and death, whom he counts among his bosom friends. The otherwise Christian is a chocolate Christian! Dissolving in water and melting at the smell of fire. "Sweeties" they are! Bonbons, lollipops! Living their lives on a glass dish or in a cardboard box, each clad in his soft clothing, a little frilled white paper to preserve his dear little delicate constitution.[1]

Like C.T. Studd, Nehemiah turned his back on the comforts afforded him in Susa. He left his stable government job in the royal court and took on the role of governor in a region that—though once the headquarters of God's people—had now become wild and desolate. Making that kind of move required serious sacrifice.

After he arrived in Israel, Nehemiah continued to display sacrificial leadership. We see it in the episode mentioned earlier, when he confronted the nobles about the loans they had made to the common people. After all, he too was part of the upper class. His financial investments were also at stake (Nehemiah 5:10), which made his command to forgive debts, waive interest, and return land that had been seized all the more remarkable (verse 11). It was a decision that directly affected him. Yet Nehemiah was willing to sacrifice his own financial opportunities for the sake of doing what was right. Then, to underscore how serious he was, Nehemiah shook out his garments and declared, "So may God shake out every man from his house and from his labor who does not keep this promise. So may he be shaken out and emptied" (verse 13 ESV).

Every leader is, at times, required to put himself at odds with the nobles or officials of his context. Such situations often entail tough decisions. There is often a significant cost to this type of courage, but it is always best to speak the truth. Samuel Goldwyn, a famous film producer and the "G" in MGM Studios, was said to quip, "I don't want any yes-men around me. I want everybody to tell me the truth even if it costs them their jobs." A wise man knows the difference between right and wrong; and a wise leader is able to act on that knowledge with decisive determination.

Nehemiah was a great example of a sacrificial leader. Though he was the governor, he did not seek to serve himself. Rather, his goal was to serve God by serving the people. His selfless approach was motivated by a righteous fear of the Lord. As he explained, "The former governors who were before me laid burdens on the people and took from them bread and wine besides forty shekels of silver; even their servants domineered the people. But I did not do so because of the fear of God" (verse 15).

One way Nehemiah showed a sacrificial spirit was with regard to his salary. As a regional governor, he was entitled to receive regular compensation for what he provided to the stability of the empire. Yet Nehemiah refused to take the paycheck. Doing so eased the financial burden on the people, since their taxes would have contributed to his salary. But the generous governor went even further—he took money out of his own pocket to help meet the needs of those around him.

Nehemiah's sacrifice was not just financial in nature. He personally worked on the wall, gave direct oversight, encouraged the people, and fought to protect them. He did not take advantage of his position for personal gain. He could have driven up taxes, burdened the people under an impossible weight of debt, seized their property, and made them his slaves. He could have taken a small group of elite leaders and made them fantastically wealthy in the wake of rebuilding Jerusalem. But he didn't. Instead, he refused to be compensated at all. He did this to help lighten the burden that weighed heavily on the people.

Nehemiah's generosity came at his own expense. Anyone can be a big spender when he's not using his own money. But Nehemiah's hospitality was sincere, paid for out of his own pocket. As he reported, "There were at my table one hundred and fifty Jews and officials, besides those who came to us from the nations that were around us" (verse 17). Meat and wine were expensive, so in order to spare the people from the burden of providing it, Nehemiah paid the bill himself. But his banquet hall was not reserved for just a few. The text says he fed over 150 people every day!

Nehemiah's leadership was exemplary in another way. He worked among the wall builders, picking up a trowel to build and a sword to defend against nearby enemies. He was on the "factory floor," so to speak. This hands-on governor did not take advantage of the building project to acquire wealth, nor did he become distracted by the work at hand and pursue personal profits. Instead, he came to the job site and remained fully focused on serving others.

Essentially Nehemiah had a big-picture idea of what needed to be done. It was not about him! He was willing to sacrifice for the greater good, and as a result he accomplished some incredible feats. His lasting legacy was not predicated on self-preservation, but on selfless service. And his courage was rooted in knowing that no matter how great the difficulties he encountered, God is greater still.

Along those lines, C.T. Studd noted the difference between real men and "chocolate" Christians. He wrote, "Difficulties, dangers, disease, death, or division don't deter any but Chocolates from executing God's will. When someone says there's a lion in the way, the real Christian promptly replies, 'That's hardly enough inducement for me; I want a bear or two besides to make it worth my while to go.'"[2] That is the kind of courage that characterized Nehemiah. Yet it's important to note this did not stem from foolish pride or immature bravado. Rather, Nehemiah's resolve was rooted in faith. He had confident trust in God and placed his full dependence upon the Lord alone.

Faith: Courage Is God-oriented

Faith is the most important element of God-exalting courage. Faith depends fully on God, making it the opposite of self-reliant pride. Courage that is motivated by pride is preoccupied with temporal accolades, personal enrichment, and the opinions of others. It worries about getting a reward in this life and on this earth. But courage that comes from faith is concerned with what God thinks. It desires only His approval and reward.

Nehemiah's sole concern was to perform his duties in keeping with the will of God. There is no indication that the people in Jerusalem fully appreciated the sacrifices he made on their behalf. Neither is there any indication that Nehemiah thought about creating a lasting monument to his greatness. He was not consumed with his own glory, but with God's. He was quick to affirm that the strength to succeed did not reside in him, but in the Lord. His courage was cultivated in private prayer, through humble dependence on the Almighty.

Nehemiah did not pray that men would recognize his accomplishments, but that God would remember him "according to all that [he had] done for this people" (5:19). In asking God to remember him, Nehemiah did not ask for help in the present situation. Rather, he looked over his completed work and asked for the divine reward that is promised by God to all who sacrificially labor in His name and for His glory. The only approval that really mattered to Nehemiah was God's. More than being great in the eyes of men, he wanted to be found faithful before the Lord.

Nehemiah further prayed that God would remember His promises to His people. He reminded the Lord of the words He had spoken through Moses: "If you return to Me and keep My commandments and do them, though those of you who have been scattered were in the most remote part of the heavens, I will gather them from there and will bring them to the place where I have chosen to cause My name to dwell" (Nehemiah 1:8). Nehemiah pleaded with God to remember that promise and bring it to fruition.

Nehemiah also called the people to remember God's faithfulness to them even when they were threatened by their enemies. Nehemiah said, "Do not be afraid of them; remember the Lord who is great and awesome, and fight for your brothers, your sons, your daughters, your wives and your houses" (4:14). Interestingly, the confluence of humble dependence and personal responsibility are seen side-by-side in that verse. On the one hand, the people were called to trust the Lord. On the other hand, they were charged to be ready for battle.

Nehemiah also asked the Lord to protect the righteous by punishing the wicked. He even mentioned some of the wicked by name—Tobiah, Sanballat, and the deceitful prophetess Noadiah. Sometimes Nehemiah encountered enemies where he least expected to find them. There were some among his own people, even among the priests, who had transgressed the law of Moses and defiled the priesthood. Nehemiah asked God to remember them (13:29). The knowledge that God would one day judge all the wicked enabled Nehemiah to lead with courage. The Lord had everything and everyone under His sovereign control, including Israel's enemies. No sinner would go unpunished because no sin could ever escape His notice.

Nehemiah's faith in God and faithfulness to God made him a courageous leader. His actions were consistently driven out of loyalty to the Lord. In the final reforms of his administration he reinstated the tithes that paid for the Levites and musicians. Afterward he prayed, "Remember me for this, O my God, and do not blot out my loyal deeds which I have performed for the house of my God and its services" (13:14).

Nehemiah showed himself similarly zealous for the Sabbath. Again, his allegiance to the Lord prompted his bold actions. The people were not observing the Sabbath as God had commanded in Exodus 20:8, so Nehemiah put an end to all commerce on that day. He even stationed his servants at the gates of Jerusalem to stop any merchants from entering the city until the Sabbath had ended. His subsequent prayer reflected his heartfelt desire to please the Lord: "For this also remember me, O my God, and have compassion on me according to the greatness of Your lovingkindness" (13:22).

When Nehemiah discovered that the Jewish priests had intermarried with pagan women, his loyalty to God ignited his passion for the purity of God's people. His response was fiery, to the point of coming to blows. His peers may have thought he was overreacting. Yet his motive was pure and his mission righteous—he was eager to protect the priesthood from all pagan defilement. After accomplishing this goal, Nehemiah once again invoked the Lord to remember him. The last words of the book form his final prayer: "Remember me, O my God, for good." As in all of his life, Nehemiah's final words were God-centered and full of faith.

THE SOURCE OF NEHEMIAH'S COURAGE

The more Nehemiah's faith was tested, the stronger it became. That's because his faith was not grounded in himself, but in God. The same should be true of us. When our hope is anchored in the Lord, we can have courage in the face of any circumstance. As the psalmist prayed, "When I am afraid, I will put my trust in You. In God, whose word I praise, in God I have put my trust; I shall not be afraid. What can mere man do to me?" (Psalm 56:3-4). Our greatest fears melt away when we consider that God is on our side (Romans 8:31).

Lining up his offense, Nehemiah would have felt the presence of danger in the immediate vicinity. But that did not stop him from staying true to the task at hand, remaining in the pocket long enough to complete the play. Armed with a God-centered faith, no fear could faze him.

Nehemiah embodies the courageous leadership of a godly man. He kept his composure in high-pressure situations and acted decisively on his convictions. He realized the cost of true leadership and served his people with sacrificial integrity. Finally, he kept his eyes on the heavenly prize, looking to the Lord for his ultimate recognition. After all, as Nehemiah knew, the empty praise of man is soon forgotten, but the reward of God will never fade away.

Real Men Love Their Wives

Lessons from the Life of Peter

RICH GREGORY

It would have been nearing midday on the Sabbath when Jesus and four of His disciples made the short walk back from the synagogue to Peter's home. The Lord had just finished teaching at the morning service, and the congregation had been astounded by both His authoritative instruction and His power over demons. When the group arrived at Peter's house, they saw that Peter's young wife was struggling to set the meal by herself because her mother was confined to bed, dreadfully sick with a fever. As the men entered the room, the buzz of excitement that hovered over the village of Capernaum stopped abruptly at the door. Jesus knew the cause, and even though it was the Sabbath, He placed the well-being of Peter's mother-in-law before the legalistic restrictions of the Jewish religious leaders. As Mark's Gospel records, "He came to her and raised her up, taking her by the hand, and the fever left her, and she waited on them" (Mark 1:31). By healing Peter's mother-in-law before the meal had even been served, Jesus ministered both to her and to Peter's wife. The young woman not only received her mother back in full health, she also got the help she needed to serve the afternoon meal.

In that act of healing, the kindness and love of Jesus was observed by at least six people in the room. Surely, none took more notice than Peter's wife. Perhaps it was difficult for her not to compare the perfect, loving character of Jesus with the brash, outspoken nature of her sinful husband. She would again witness the Lord's merciful compassion that evening. As dusk began to fall, Jesus stood on the doorstep of her house and healed those who had been waiting all day in accordance with Sabbath law. Though Jesus was tired from teaching that morning, He was still willing to take the time to show tender care for the multitude that had gathered around. Indeed, it was easy to see that in comparison to Christ, Peter (and everyone else, for that matter) fell far short.

In the Gospels, Scripture reveals Peter as a bold, rather impulsive man who repeatedly overstepped the bounds of verbal propriety. His blunt tongue was often the subject of Christ's loving admonition. When Peter boasted that he would forgive his brother "up to seven times," Jesus lovingly corrected him: "I do not say to you, up to seven times, but up to seventy times seven" (Matthew 18:21-22). When the overconfident disciple's faith faltered in the midst of a severe storm on the Sea of Galilee, Jesus took his hand and said firmly, "You of little faith, why did you doubt?" (Matthew 14:31). The most brazen display of Peter's brashness was when he audaciously rebuked Jesus for talking about His impending crucifixion. The Lord's response cut him to the quick: "You are a stumbling block to Me; for you are not setting your mind on God's interests, but man's" (Matthew 16:23). From just these few examples, we can see clearly that Peter was not a laid-back, soft-spoken fisherman. Though he loved the Lord deeply, he was also aggressive, impetuous, and thickheaded.

Peter lived in a world that viewed women as inferior to men. The rabbinic statement "Blessed art thou, O Lord our God, who has not made me a woman" summarized the chauvinism that was widespread in his day. It's very likely Peter would have been influenced by the attitudes and prejudices of his male-dominated society. Given Peter's personality and the prevailing cultural bias, it's not hard to see the potential for difficulty in Peter's marriage relationship.

Like most men who have good intentions, Peter undoubtedly loved his wife, but he did not really understand what that was supposed to look like. At least not yet. Jesus, who would become the model of biblical love in Peter's life, was just beginning His ministry—which meant the headstrong disciple still had a lot to learn. The incredible healing of Peter's mother-in-law was one of Christ's earlier miracles. On that unforgettable day, Peter's wife may have asked herself a question that many wives have been asking ever since: *Why can't my husband be more like Jesus?*

But over the next few years, Peter would be changed. He was transformed by the love of Christ—a love that humbled his pride, softened his rough edges, forgave his sin, and saved his soul. No one would have felt the wonder of that transformation more dramatically than Peter's wife. By the end of Peter's apostolic ministry, she was not only traveling with him (1 Corinthians 9:5), but his love for her had developed to the point that he was able to instruct other men on what it meant to truly love their wives. In 1 Peter 3:7, the softened apostle, writing under the guidance of the Holy Spirit and from his own life experience, gave the following command: "You husbands in the same way, live with your wives in an understanding way, as with someone weaker, since she is a woman; and show her honor as a fellow heir of the grace of life, so that your prayers will not be hindered."

Having learned the true definition of love from Christ Himself, Peter succinctly expressed a lifetime of marital wisdom in that one verse. He wrote to encourage Christian husbands with a profound reminder that real men love their wives. And in order to do that, they must demonstrate both *understanding* and *honor*.

UNDERSTANDING—WHAT HUSBANDS MUST KNOW

Peter began his instruction to Christian husbands with this short command: "Live with your wives in an understanding way."

Translated more literally the phrase reads, "Dwell together with your wives according to knowledge." What knowledge is the apostle referring to? The answer is all-encompassing and has two aspects: Husbands must *know* their wives, and they must also *know* the Lord.

First, the Christian husband is called to understand his wife. He must put forth the effort to know her personality, character, needs, and desires. This requires an investment in the most basic building blocks of a relationship—from paying attention to listening well to showing a sincere interest in her and her well-being. And second, the husband is called to know God and His Word. It is the knowledge of God that allows the husband to relate to his wife in such a way that God's ways are made known to her. Only a husband who knows both his Bible and his wife beyond a superficial level will be able to effectively shepherd her toward godliness.

God's primary purpose in marriage is that both the husband and the wife grow in sanctification through their love for Him and one another. In this, the husband has been given a leading role. The apostle Paul explained that truth in Ephesians 5:25-33, a passage that is parallel to 1 Peter 3:7. There, Paul wrote, "Husbands, love your wives, just as Christ also loved the church and gave Himself up for her, so that He might sanctify her" (verses 25-26). A husband's love for his wife ought to reflect Christ's love for the church; and the Lord's affection for His bride is both sacrificial and purifying. As one author has explained about these verses:

> Love wants only the best for the one it loves, and it cannot bear for a loved one to be corrupted or misled by anything evil or harmful. When a husband's love for his wife is like Christ's love for His church, he will continually seek to help purify her from any sort of defilement. He will seek to protect her from the world's contamination and protect her holiness, virtue, and purity in every way. He will never induce her to do that which is wrong or unwise or expose her to that which is less than good.[1]

The Christian husband is called to lead his wife in holiness, shepherding her in biblical wisdom and protecting her from worldly influences. He does this by pursuing God's purpose for marriage, encouraging his wife in her walk with Christ, and creating an environment in which she can grow spiritually. Of course, that begins with his own private devotion. His life ought to be a model of godliness such that his wife is drawn to the beauty of Christ that she sees daily displayed in him.

When spiritual growth is the goal, there is no place for angry words or inconsiderate actions. Those kinds of sinful behavior, though common of many husbands, do not honor God's purpose for marriage. The godly husband, who understands both his wife and God's Word, responds with patience and acts with purpose. His goal is to lead her in godliness by showing her the love of Christ. That love is both selfless and sanctifying.

Peter's command to "live with your wives in an understanding way" is followed by an explanation as to why this is so important: "as with someone weaker, since she is a woman." At first glance that phrase may sound demeaning and derogatory. But in fact, it is exactly the opposite. The apostle was not suggesting that women are emotionally or intellectually inferior to their husbands. Rather, he was observing that wives are in a position of weakness, and therefore need to be protected. Physically, they are generally not as strong as their husbands. Spiritually, they are fully equal in Christ yet they are called to submit to their husband's leadership (Ephesians 5:22). Culturally, in the society to which Peter wrote, women were often denigrated. It was not uncommon in ancient Roman culture for husbands to dominate, subjugate, or even physically abuse their wives. Hence Peter's countercultural command to first-century husbands would have been unmistakable: "Never use your physical strength, God-given authority, or social status to take advantage of your wife. Do not exploit your position of strength. Rather, live with your wife in a way that demonstrates genuine care and understanding." This reminder is still greatly needed in Christian marriages today (cf. Colossians 3:19), as husbands remember that the submissiveness of their wives is a beautiful reflection of Christ's humility before God the Father (Philippians 2:3-8).

The caring husband uses his strength not to harm his wife but to *protect* and *provide for* her. This goes beyond merely physical protection and material provision to every arena of life. Financially, the husband is responsible to care for his wife by working hard and making fiscally responsible decisions. Emotionally, he is to take the time to listen to her and remind her of his love. Spiritually, he is to prayerfully watch for error and temptation not only in his own life, but also in hers. Culturally, he is to guard his home against the infiltration of ungodly influences, whether from unwise friendships or worldly entertainment. In all of this a husband is to seek his wife's best—showing her the love of Christ through his own selfless service. For the Christian husband, protecting his wife goes far beyond simply walking next to her on the edge of the sidewalk that is closest to the street.

HONOR—WHAT HUSBANDS MUST SHOW

Peter's admonition to husbands continues with a second directive: "Show her honor as a fellow heir of the grace of life, so that your prayers will not be hindered." Not only are husbands commanded to *understand* their wives, they are also called to *honor* them. In a society where women were often treated as second-class citizens, Peter exhorted Christian husbands to act differently. "Don't demean your wife," he told them. "Honor her." The godly husband neither scorns nor mistreats his wife. Rather, he respects her as his dearest companion and cherishes her as a gift from God. As Paul wrote in Ephesians 5:28-29, "Husbands ought also to love their own wives as their own bodies. He who loves his own wife loves himself; for no one ever hated his own flesh, but nourishes and cherishes it, just as Christ also does the church."

Peter's description of the Christian wife as "a fellow heir of the grace of life" would have reminded his readers that both husband and wife are on equal footing before Christ. Men should treat their wives accordingly, recognizing that "wives, like husbands, believe in the same Savior, are redeemed by the same ransom, live by the same grace, and look forward to the same eternal destiny."[2] One day they will both stand before the Lord, where each will receive the promised inheritance of eternal reward (cf. 1 Peter 1:4). The husband, in particular, will give an account for the way in which he shepherded his wife. He is the leader of the home, and it is his joyful responsibility to point her toward Christ until the time she meets her Savior face to face in heaven.

At the end of verse 7, Peter added one last motivating reminder: "so that your prayers will not be hindered." What a sobering admonition! When a husband defaults upon his obligation to properly love his wife, he is rejecting the model of love that God has put forward in the person of Jesus Christ. As Peter had learned, the demonstration of the love of Christ is the cornerstone upon which one's relationship with God is founded. Peter's point was that a husband's refusal to demonstrate that same love is hypocrisy, and it directly affects his fellowship with God. As one commentator wrote,

> No more serious divine threat could be given to a believer than that—the interruption of all the promises of prayers heard and answered (cf. John 14:13-14). That is severe, cutting off the divine blessing, which shows how critical is Christian husbands' loving care of their partners in this grace of life.[3]

That reminder is a serious warning to any man who might be tempted to abuse the leadership role God has given him.

REFLECTING THE LOVE OF CHRIST

As Peter discovered over the course of his life, real men love their wives in a way that reflects the love of Christ. They do so by living with their wives in an understanding way and by showing them honor and kindness. The result of that kind of love is not just a happy marriage, but one that brings glory to God.

The responsibility given to the husband should not be undertaken lightly. It is a call to shepherd, provide, protect, and lead. It requires love, self-sacrifice, humility, and diligence. Ultimately, it looks to heaven and purposes to live each day in light of that future inheritance. In the meantime, it rests in the grace of God—knowing that the best of human relationships can be fully enjoyed only in light of our fellowship with Him.

Though filled with responsibility, a marriage founded on Christlike love is a profound blessing and an incredible gift from God. The inevitable result is joyous spiritual union that goes beyond the physical and emotional realms. No human relationship is deeper or closer than a Christian marriage—as husband and wife walk together in love, stepping through life in unison before their Creator and Savior.

Of course, no husband can live as God intended unless he has first experienced the transforming love of Christ. Salvation is the starting point for all true love. Peter certainly understood this fact. Before he met Jesus, he didn't understand the nature of love, forgiveness, humility, or sacrifice. He was rough, brash, hardheaded, and outspoken. But as he came to know the Savior, he saw love personified and his life began to change.

But Peter would not fully understand the depths of love until the cross. On that unforgettable day, only a few hours after Peter had denied Him, the Savior died to pay for Peter's sins—and not just for his sins, but for the sins of all who would believe. The love of Christ, demonstrated at Calvary, revolutionized Peter's life forever. After the resurrection, he would be restored by Jesus (John 21:15-23) and empowered for dramatic Christian service (cf. Acts 1–12). Several decades later, as he wrote to encourage the believers in Asia Minor, he paused briefly to remind husbands how they ought to love their wives. Having experienced the love of Christ, Peter instructed his readers to reflect that same love in their marriages.

THE TRANSFORMING POWER OF CHRIST

Nearly 40 years had passed since that memorable day in Capernaum when Peter's wife must have wished her husband was more like Jesus. So much had happened since then. Peter had been radically transformed by the Lord and used mightily to lead the church. His wife had witnessed his incredible transformation from a coarse fisherman to a godly man and a loving husband. It had taken place as she ministered with him in cities like Jerusalem, Antioch, and Rome.

Now the faithful apostle was about to die as a martyr for Christ. Church tradition tells us that, even at this dramatic moment, his wife was still there with him. As Peter was being prepared by the executioners for his impending death, his wife, also slated for execution, was led in front of him. According to Clement of Alexandria, a second-century church leader, "We are told that when blessed Peter saw his wife led away to death he was glad that her call had come and that she was returning home, and spoke to her in the most encouraging and comforting tones, addressing her by name: 'My dear, remember the Lord.'"[4]

Peter was then taken and nailed to a cross, on which he would spill his blood as a witness to the gospel. Not feeling worthy to die in the same manner as Christ, he asked to be crucified upside down.[5] As Peter's wife caught one last glimpse of him, she no longer saw a man selfishly focused upon his own desires, motivations, and plans. Instead, she saw her loving husband willingly dying for the sake of his Lord, calming her fears and encouraging her to stay faithful to the very end.

Her old thoughts of *Why can't he love the way Jesus loved?* would have become such a sweet memory, a monument to the transforming power of Christ. Even in the moments before they died, Peter reminded her of the love of Christ. Soon they would both be in glory. They were "returning home," as he had sweetly called her to remember. With those final words, he had faithfully fulfilled his duty to love his wife as every Christian husband should—by leading her more and more toward Christ until the day she went to heaven. Soon they would be rewarded as coheirs of the promised inheritance.

After Peter's heart stopped beating and he stepped into glory, his lifelong transformation was complete. And as he stood in sinless perfection in the presence of his Savior, Peter finally understood the reality of love to its fullest degree.

Real Men Shepherd Their Families

Lessons from Ephesians 5–6

JIM PILE

R ecently our family gathered around the dinner table to sing "Happy Birthday" to our oldest daughter. It was hard to believe she was already 24. As we sang, I couldn't help but think about all the Lord had taught me through the years about being a father. Two dozen years earlier, as a new dad, I had no idea how much I needed to learn or how much this little bundle of joy would teach me about parenting.

Perhaps the greatest lesson I needed to learn is that the mission field starts at home. In Matthew 28:19-20, Jesus told His followers, "Go therefore and make disciples of all the nations, baptizing them in the name of the Father and the Son and the Holy Spirit, teaching them to observe all that I commanded you." The command to make disciples not only relates to world missions, it also applies directly to the family. That is where the making of disciples must start—in the home. And that is why shepherding our children is so important. After all, the family is God's instrument for passing on faith, righteousness, and truth from one generation to the next (Deuteronomy 4:9; 6:4-7).

So how do we make sure we're shepherding our families as we should? What can we do to effectively train up our children in the nurture and admonition of the Lord? The answer begins with our own sanctification. Our parenting is a reflection of our personal walk with Christ. Thus, before we can grow as fathers, we need to make sure we're growing in obedience to our heavenly Father. That happens as we put off the deeds of the flesh and put on the mind of Christ (Ephesians 4:22-24).

In the first half of this chapter we will look at some of the sins that commonly manifest themselves in family relationships. Then, in the second half, we will consider several keys to building a strong foundation for godliness in your parenting. Let's begin by considering three "parent traps" or temptations that Christian fathers frequently face.

SINS THAT HURT FAMILY RELATIONSHIPS

Parent Trap #1: *Pride*

The greatest sin men struggle with is pride. It is the foundational vice of all other sins, and it can manifest itself in our family relationships in countless ways. Even as believers redeemed from sin, we will find ourselves continually doing battle against pride (Romans 7:15-21). In fact, we can demonstrate pride without even realizing it. As one person noted, "Pride is the first shirt we put on in the morning and the last one we take off at night." It is a pervasive problem that we must take seriously—we must mortify its presence in our lives before we can properly relate to God and each other (1 Peter 5:5).

For most men, there are a number of "classic" ways pride can show up in family relationships. Sometimes it manifests itself in ways specific to marriage or parenting, like failing to live with one's wife in an understanding way (1 Peter 3:7) or responding with an attitude of irritation or impatience toward one's children. At other times pride evidences itself in a more general way—perhaps through an overly competitive spirit, a judgmental disposition, discontentment, self-pity, or people pleasing.

Significantly, pride can also manifest itself in an unwillingness to ask for forgiveness. Some men have the attitude that they can do no wrong, and they demand obedience from their wives and children by issuing abrupt commands like, "Do as you're told!" They rule over their families with a dictatorial hand that suppresses honest feedback. Their children won't open up because, as they would say, "If Dad never admits when he is wrong, why should I talk to him?" That type of heavy-handed arrogance creates an atmosphere of hypocrisy in the home and bitterness in the family. Children who grow up in homes like that will not see their need for Christ because they observe a false standard of righteousness (1 John 2:4). A truly humble father, by contrast, makes it clear that he is a sinner saved by grace, and that he is fully dependent on Christ and His righteousness.

As a practical pride-killing exercise, ask your wife to identify the biggest spiritual issue in your life that she would like to see you work on, and then get to work on it (1 Timothy 4:7-8). Slaying the sin of pride in your life is critical to being able to truly enjoy God-honoring relationships. It is important to never forget that God is opposed to the proud and gives His grace to the humble (Proverbs 3:34; James 4:6).

Parent Trap #2: Preoccupation

Over the years as a pastor, I have seen many men become lazy and undisciplined in regard to both their relationship with the Lord and their responsibility to shepherd the family. That negligence often stems from a sinful preoccupation—as careers, hobbies, entertainment, or other personal pursuits are given unbalanced attention. In the process, the family is neglected. And the end result is disastrous.

A man's sinful preoccupation will lead to increased isolation from his wife and children. Over time those relationships will deteriorate, and may be lost completely. Years later, with his family in shambles, the negligent man looks at the aftermath and wonders, *How did this happen?* Tragically, he is the primary culprit. Having never made the necessary effort to develop strong family ties, he finds himself all alone with nothing but his empty pursuits to comfort him. But at that point it is too late. The damage is already done.

The sad reality is that many men are not willing to take the time to invest themselves, spiritually and relationally, into their wives and their children. They don't want to make the effort to shepherd their families, so they shirk their God-given responsibilities. We have all seen surveys that talk about the minute or two that the average American father spends with his kids each day. When men pursue their own interests at the expense of their families, their children are inevitably raised by someone or something else (for example, computers or television). Even Christian families are not immune. Dad can become so consumed with his work or his favorite pastime that he is seldom home. When he is, he makes work-related phone calls, watches television, or surfs the Internet. Meanwhile, his wife and kids are screaming for attention while he remains oblivious—lost in his own little world—until his family falls apart. As Christian fathers, we must not allow patterns of preoccupation to rob us of time with our families.

Parent Trap #3: Anger

Impatience, irritation, frustration, and harsh speech are all indicative of an angry heart—a heart that is quick to "fight and quarrel" (James 4:2) when it does not get what it wants. Anger is a form of self-worship—the person who is angry refuses to tolerate any person or circumstance that does not conform to his selfish desires or directives. He takes every offense personally, and often reacts forcefully and sometimes even violently. But, as Scripture teaches us, "the anger of man does not achieve the righteousness of God" (James 1:20).

Oftentimes a man is tempted to become angry when he feels like his wife or children are not responding to him the way he thinks they should. His unmet expectations stir up his emotions, and he gets mad. Though the visible manifestation of anger can look very different—from uncontrolled outbursts to manipulative silent treatments—its sinful root is all the same. The godly husband and father works hard to put off anger while simultaneously putting on its opposite, the fruit of the Spirit—love, joy, peace, patience, kindness, goodness, faithfulness, gentleness, and self-control (Galatians 5:22-23).

We must not forget that given our place as head of the family, our children observe and learn from what we model. When we make a habit of rationalizing our anger (by saying things like, "I wasn't angry; I was just being firm" or "I wouldn't get so upset if you didn't _____!"), we teach our children that anger is excusable. But sinful anger is never justified—no matter what your spouse says or how disobedient the kids are. If patterns of anger are allowed to develop over time, the results can be devastating for the family.

Consider the example of a man named Tom, is a professing Christian in a typical evangelical church in America. He has been married to his childhood sweetheart for eight years, and they have three children. God has blessed Tom with a good-paying job and a comfortable home, and he serves as a Sunday school teacher in his church. From the outside it appears that he is living the American dream. Yet beneath this veneer of success there is a longstanding problem of impatience and anger toward his wife. And when Tom doesn't get the results that he wants—like the approval of his boss, his wife's affection, or his children's obedience—he erupts. For his wife and children, it is like living at the foot of an active volcano.

What Tom is teaching his children by his angry, self-centered lifestyle is that the only way to solve problems is to win at any cost. It doesn't matter to him who gets hurt in the process because he is focused on controlling everything in his life. Children growing up under that type of leadership are deprived of the biblical resources necessary to peacefully resolve disagreements and conflicts (Colossians 3:12-15). Moreover, they are daily exposed to a glaring inconsistency between how their father behaves at church and how he behaves at home. That kind of hypocrisy is often a stumbling block to their reception of the gospel.

FROM TRAPS TO TRUTH

How do you "put to death" sins like pride, preoccupation, and anger? First, repent and turn from your sin. Confess it to the Lord and to those you have offended, acknowledging the wrongdoing and taking full responsibility for it (Proverbs 28:13; 1 John 1:9). Second, commit yourself to making godly choices in the future. Ask others to hold you accountable as you fight against specific temptations (Psalm 119:106). Third, renew your mind through the faithful study of God's Word. Meditate continually on His truth (Joshua 1:8; 1 Peter 2:2). And finally, walk in the power of the Holy Spirit by submitting to His Word (cf. Ephesians 5:18 with Colossians 3:16) and seeking to humbly serve others (Galatians 6:16-24; Philippians 2:3-4).

WAYS TO STRENGTHEN
FAMILY RELATIONSHIPS

Up to this point we've considered some of the most common problem areas for Christian fathers. Now let's look at some keys to building a strong foundation for our family relationships.

A man once asked his pastor, "What makes a good marriage?" The pastor replied, "The answer, my friend, is simple: What makes a good Christian marriage is two obedient Christians." That is so true. If you are saved and walking in the Spirit, then your family relationships can thrive no matter what trials or hardships you experience.

If we are to be godly men, it is imperative for us to focus on what

God calls us to do. We should seek to live out His commands joyfully, consistently, and without hesitation. Let's begin by considering the Lord's command, "Husbands, love your wives" (Ephesians 5:25).

Love Your Wife

We will touch on this subject only briefly because it was already addressed in the previous chapter. Yet this divine command to husbands is so incredibly significant it bears repeating. We are called to love our wives.

Apart from your relationship to Christ, your marriage is the most important relationship you have. It should be the primary relationship in your home (Genesis 2:24; Matthew 19:6; 1 Peter 3:7). My wife and I often reminded our kids while they were growing up that they were welcome members of our family but not the center of it. As one pastor wisely remarked at the conclusion of his own son's wedding, "What God has brought together let no man separate. Let no one come between you—especially your children." That is an exhortation every married couple needs to hear.

Even after children are born, the marital relationship is still primary. In that regard, one of the most important lessons a father can teach his children is to honor their mother. Before he leaves for work, he might want to remind them to obey her while he is gone, saying something like, "That is my beautiful wife and your precious mother that you need to serve today while I'm at work, and you will treat her with your utmost honor and respect while I'm not here or you will answer to me when I get home" (see Ephesians 6:2).

The greatest gift you can give your children is to love your wife in a way that models the love of Christ (Colossians 3:19). They should see your kind words and sacrificial deeds toward her and think, *Someday I want to have a marriage just like mom and dad's.* Make sure you show appropriate affection toward your wife in front of your children so that they see biblical love in action. Our adult kids still roll their eyes when I give their mother a kiss in front of them. But despite their silly protests, it lets them see how much we still love each other after nearly 30 years of marriage. And that gives them a sense of security within our family.

Nourish and cherish your wife (Ephesians 5:29) by tenderly providing for her needs, serving her sacrificially, helping her grow spiritually, giving her comfort and security in times of trial, and treating her as a beloved companion (Proverbs 31:11). Moreover, set the right example of humility in your home by being transparent with your wife. Demonstrate your love by confessing your sins when you blow it with her. This is beneficial to your children as well, because they need to see what humility looks like in action. A truly humble man who walks in integrity makes it easier for his wife and children to follow in his footsteps (Proverbs 20:7).

Finally, continue to practice living with your wife in "an understanding way" (1 Peter 3:7). That truth is crucial to loving her and takes a lifetime of maximum effort. It means to dwell with her according to knowledge. Such knowledge includes knowing your wife and knowing the Scriptures so that you may instruct her regarding the truths of God's Word (1 Corinthians 14:35).

One of the finest examples of this I ever observed was a couple at Grace Community Church who both lived into their nineties before they died. They were married for 70 years! As I visited them in their home they would hold hands and look at each other as if they were still in their twenties. Their love was as vibrant for each other after 70 years as it was when they were just starting out. Why? The wife told me it was because her husband applied the command of living with her in "an understanding way" for all those 70 years. What a testimony! He was a real example of what godly manhood looks like in marriage.

Love Your Children

After the apostle Paul commanded husbands to love their wives, he began the very next chapter in Ephesians with instructions for

Christian parents. In Ephesians 6:4, he encouraged fathers with these words: "Do not provoke your children to anger, but bring them up in the discipline and instruction of the Lord." If we truly love our children, we will be faithful to bring them up according to biblical principles. The mission field really does start in the home. But outside of formal teaching times, how can we practically love and teach our children? Let's look at a four important ways we can accomplish this.

1. Through Your Example

The single most important way you can shepherd your children is by modeling your love for Christ in everyday life (Matthew 22:37-38). As Jesus explained in the Sermon on the Mount, "Let your light shine before men in such a way that they may see your good works, and glorify your Father who is in heaven" (Matthew 5:16). Remember that you are a Christian man first, even before you are a husband and father, and your daily reliance on God's amazing grace will speak volumes to your children (Luke 9:23; Ephesians 2:8-10). The old adage "There is more caught than taught" applies directly to your family. They are deeply influenced by how you live your life.

In light of that sobering fact, let them see that "the love of Christ controls" you (2 Corinthians 5:14). Demonstrate what it means to "walk by the Spirit" and no longer carry out the "desires of the flesh" (Galatians 5:16-25). Display the character of a righteous man to them. There is no room for hypocrisy in your life, especially as a father. Children can see right through any kind of inconsistency. So make sure your life matches your profession. As Solomon wrote in Proverbs 20:7, "A righteous man who walks in his integrity—how blessed are his sons after him."

2. Through Life Situations

Teaching your children should occur in the milieu of your everyday life, both inside and outside the home (Deuteronomy 6:6-7).

Successes, failures, trials, illnesses, school problems, and relationship issues—the normal circumstances of life—all present valuable opportunities for spiritual instruction. Life is a classroom that you can use to lead your children to God and His Word every day (Proverbs 1:1-7).

A few years ago three of my children and I were on our way back to our church after eating lunch at a local restaurant with a friend of our family. Without any warning, we were suddenly hit by another car. Everyone was all right, but it was a scary experience for us. Later I asked my children what they had learned from the accident. My son exclaimed, "Not to go to lunch with Mr. Smith." My oldest daughter chimed in, "I learned not to be a passenger in any car you're driving." My other daughter thought about it and said, "We have to be careful and trust God." Thank goodness we had one theologian in the bunch! The accident ended up being a wonderful opportunity for our family to talk about biblical truth. We were able to rehearse the fact that our circumstances can literally change in the blink of an eye, which is why we must trust God with our lives at all times (James 4:14; Proverbs 3:5-6).

3. Through Questions and Answers

Whenever the opportunity arises, it is important to ask thought-provoking questions of your children and then help them think through their responses from a biblical point of view (2 Timothy 3:15-17). This will teach them to pause and think about what God would have them do in a particular situation as they are confronted with the trials and temptations of life (Proverbs 14:15). In addition, be prepared as a parent for your children to ask you many thought-provoking questions (cf. Exodus 12:26-27). Your children's natural curiosity will create wonderful opportunities for you to teach them spiritual truth. Encouraging your children to ask good questions will not only help them develop mentally and spiritually, but will also challenge you to sharpen your own theological acumen.

Always try to be available to listen to their thoughts and answer their questions and concerns. Mealtimes, bedtime, and travel times are especially good opportunities for you to help your children think about their day and reflect on their relationship to God. Many years ago, on our way home from church, our oldest daughter saw a plane flying in the sky and asked me, "Dad, if God is everywhere, is that plane going to hit God?" After some initial laughter from all of us in the car, her question led to a good discussion about the Lord's omnipresence and the nature of God as Spirit (John 4:24; Colossians 1:15).

4. THROUGH FAMILY ACTIVITIES

When I ask people in strong families what makes them strong, doing enjoyable things together is mentioned again and again—activities such as doing ministry, eating meals, working on projects, going on vacation, spending time outdoors, developing family traditions, attending each other's special events, and enjoying "family nights" together. Generally speaking, happy families are those that do things together because they understand that strong relationships develop during those times.

Parents sometimes wonder whether quality time or quantity time is more important. May I suggest that it is *quality time* with your family in *great quantity*? The two are inseparable. Give your family as much time as you can; and do your best not to waste a moment of it. As one Christian father confessed,

> My family's all grown and the kids are all gone. But if I had to do it all over again, this is what I would do. I would love my wife more in front of my children. I would laugh with my children more—at our mistakes and our joys. I would listen more, even to the littlest child. I would be more honest about my own weaknesses, never pretending perfection. I would pray differently for my family; instead of focusing on them, I'd focus on me.

I would do more things together with my children. I would encourage them more and bestow more praise. I would pay more attention to little things, like deeds and words of thoughtfulness. And then, finally, if I had to do it all over again, I would share God more intimately with my family; every ordinary thing that happened in every ordinary day I would use to direct them to God.[1]

THE BLESSINGS OF FAITHFULNESS

It has been said, "If your Christianity isn't working at home, don't export it." What a convicting thought! Our godly example must start with those who know us best. As Christian men, we are called to love the Lord first and foremost, and then to love the members of our families as ourselves (Matthew 22:37-40). That love compels us to lead them in Christlikeness and serve them with humility and care.

Faithful parenting has great rewards, both for this life and the next. Putting biblical principles into practice and guiding our families in the fear and admonition of the Lord will allow us to experience the profound joys of Psalm 128. There we read,

> How blessed is everyone who fears the LORD, who walks in His ways. When you shall eat of the fruit of your hands, you will be happy and it will be well with you. Your wife shall be like a fruitful vine within your house, your children like olive plants around your table. Behold, for thus shall the man be blessed who fears the LORD (verses 1-4).

May you and your loved ones enjoy the riches of that promise as you daily walk with Christ and shepherd your family according to His Word.

12

Real Men Work Hard
Lessons from the Book of Proverbs

AUSTIN DUNCAN

I'd like to tell you about a man you may have met before. His parents are ashamed of him, and he lives in constant frustration and misery. He continually runs out of money, always teetering on the brink of complete insolvency. He has real, immediate needs but is unable to meet them, which is why he has trouble sleeping at night. It's strange, though, because he sleeps just fine during the day—waking up late, hitting the snooze button, and rolling back onto his pillow. If he ever left the house he would be instantly confronted by his negative reputation; or worse, a lion in the streets. That's right, a lion. Well, not an actual lion. You see, this guy loves to make up excuses, real and imagined, to avoid going to work. He thinks work is a curse, but those who know him think he is a curse. In fact, some people say they would rather drink vinegar or have smoke blown in their eyes than be around this guy. His standing in the community is really that bad. He is an unwelcome freeloader and an unreliable fool. You've probably heard about him. Most people have. His is known as "the sluggard," and his reckless life is depicted in the book of Proverbs.

INTRODUCING THE SLUGGARD

The man we have just described is not a hero but a villain. For that matter, he is not a man at all—rather, he's a child in a grown-up body. Throughout Proverbs he is referred to as a fool, a lazy man, a slacker, and a sluggard. He is indolent, irresponsible, immature, and headed for impending ruin. His unproductive life yields nothing of value except to serve as a warning for others not to follow down his path. Anyone who wishes to honor God in how he lives—as a diligent, disciplined, and dutiful man—will do well to pay attention and take heed.

The book of Proverbs is ideal for Christian men to study. It is an instruction manual written from a father to his son describing what it means to live skillfully and in a way that pleases God. Throughout its pages, Solomon covers a wide range of topics—including financial stewardship, marriage, friendship, discipline, and work. His teaching is immensely practical as he endeavors to guide his son toward wisdom and away from foolishness.

So let's consider Solomon's teaching as he unfolds one of the most important characteristics of a godly man. Real men avoid the folly of laziness. Or conversely, *real men work hard.*

IN THE BEGINNING, GOD MADE WORK

From the outset, the sluggard fails to acknowledge that work is a gift from God. Apparently he's never read Genesis 1 and 2. The opening chapters of the Bible make it clear that God Himself is a God who works. Genesis 2:2-3 is explicit in this regard: "By the seventh day God completed His work which He had done, and He rested on the seventh day from all His work which He had done. Then God blessed the seventh day and sanctified it, because it in He rested from all His work which God had created and made." After creation, God took a day of rest. But it was preceded by six days of work.

Man was created in God's image, and he is called to work too.

Adam was given certain tasks to perform in Eden, such as subduing the earth (Genesis 1:27-28) and cultivating the garden (Genesis 2:15). Notice that he was assigned these responsibilities *before* sin entered the world. His work was not a result of the fall or the curse. Granted, work—like all of life—was negatively impacted by the curse. Now it includes thistles, thorns, and the sweat of our brow (Genesis 3:18-19). But that doesn't make work evil, even if it makes it harder. Though we now live in a fallen world, God has still endorsed the inherent value of work. It was His design for human beings at creation, and it still is today.

To help us fulfill our divine mandate to work, God created us with an internal motivation system: hunger. As Proverbs 16:26 explains, "A worker's appetite works for him, for his hunger urges him on." Food and work were made to go together. These verses explain why we have to *make* a sandwich. No matter what kind of sandwich we're talking about, it has to be assembled. Look beyond our modern supermarket and we remember that hogs had to be raised and butchered, and that grain had to be harvested, milled, and baked. Vegetables were grown; cheese was processed; trucks were dispatched. A lot of work went into that lunch. It is wise to acknowledge this relationship between food and work, whether our work directly produced the food or simply provided its procurement.

By divine design, if we want to meet the most basic necessities of life, such as putting food on the table, we must be willing to work. Proverbs 12:11 puts it this way: "He who tills his land will have plenty of bread, but he who pursues worthless things lacks sense." That's why Paul's automatic assumption when dealing with slackers in the New Testament church was the very proverbial, "If anyone is not willing to work, then he is not to eat, either" (2 Thessalonians 3:10).

LAZINESS IS PRODUCTIVE TOO

Of course, work isn't the only thing that pays. According to the book of Proverbs, laziness has its own wages—namely, total ruin. "In all labor there is profit, but mere talk leads only to poverty" (Proverbs 14:23). A life of lethargy is not without consequences. Carefully consider the following fruits of being a sluggard. If you indulge in a life of laziness you will…

- Be an embarrassment to your parents (Proverbs 10:1,5)
- Live a life of frustration (13:4)
- Experience deep poverty and real need (6:6-11)
- Have a horrible reputation (10:26)
- Struggle in meaningless rest (26:14)
- Serve as a warning to others—instead of heeding the proverbs you become one (24:30)
- Leave a legacy of unfinished projects (12:27)
- Be known for your lame excuses (22:13)
- Be a source of irritation to others (10:26)
- Suffer through life in a downward spiral (13:4; 19:15)
- Endure a hard and unpleasant existence (15:19; 20:17)
- One day experience death and hell (9:16-18; 21:25)

Clearly, laziness is a serious sin accompanied by devastating consequences. A life of frustration, sorrow, and pain awaits the slothful man. Fathers are wise to teach their sons the dangers of laziness and the value of hard work. There is tremendous value in manual labor, especially for instructing young men, as they learn to equate paychecks with sweat, sunburns, and calluses. In a world of television shows, video games, social media, and other electronic distractions, laziness has never been more entertaining. But the wise man will keep his recreation in check, being diligent to work hard and take care of his responsibilities first.

OF BUGS AND SLUGS

In one of the most vivid sections of Proverbs, a simple insect becomes the lazy man's teacher. Listen to Solomon's colorful description:

> Go to the ant, O sluggard, observe her ways and be wise, which, having no chief, officer or ruler, prepares her food in the summer and gathers her provision in the harvest. How long will you lie down, O sluggard? When will you arise from your sleep? "A little sleep, a little slumber, a little folding of the hands to rest"—your poverty will come in like a vagabond, and your need like an armed man (Proverbs 6:6-11).

The lazy man's condition is so pathetic he needs to be schooled by a bug! In his timeless commentary on this passage, Charles Bridges writes, "Yet what a proof it is of the degradation of the fall, that 'man, created in the image of God,' and made wiser than the creation (Genesis 1:26; Job 35:11), should be sent, as here, to this insignificant school for instruction!"[1]

But how much the sluggard could learn if he would only study the ant. Ants do not need to be micromanaged. They do not require the constant supervision that the sluggard needs. Though they are mere insects, ants understand the inherent value of work. Unlike the lazy man, they never show up late to the office. No one has to remind them when their lunch break is over, or reprimand them for surfing the Web during work hours. Ants are always diligent. And as a result, they are always prepared for the future. They are ready when the winter comes because they have carefully stored up an ample food supply. But the sluggard ignores the future to his own peril. His poor work ethic sends him to the poorhouse. Abject poverty overcomes him swiftly and violently, "like a vagabond" or "an armed man" (verse 11). Thus the sluggard meets his own demise. Having slept for far too long, he now sleeps in a bed of his own making.

Ants don't need to read Proverbs 6. They already get it. They were created to work hard and do so without supervision. And that is Solomon's point: We too were created to work hard. When we slack off, we show how far our sin has taken us from Eden.

SINGING THE WORKPLACE BLUES

A recent study indicates that:

- Only 45 percent of Americans are satisfied in the workplace, which is the lowest level of job satisfaction in 22 years.
- Only 51 percent of people find their jobs interesting.
- Among those under age 25, 64 percent of employees say they are unhappy at work.[2]

To statistics like these the sluggard offers a hearty "Amen." He hates work and finds no joy in it. But he is missing the point entirely.

There is great reward in working hard. And it goes beyond just getting a paycheck. The godly man can take satisfaction in his work—not because work is the source of satisfaction, but because the godly man connects his daily labor to God's high calling and purpose for his life. When we "do [our] work heartily as for the Lord" (Colossians 3:23), we can find joy in whatever task we are called to perform. Thus Solomon could say, "A man will be satisfied with good by the fruit of his words, and the deeds of a man's hands will return to him" (Proverbs 12:14). Christian men should never look for ultimate meaning and fulfillment in their jobs; they should find that in Christ. We may get a paycheck from our employer, but we will one day receive a final evaluation and reward from the Lord Himself.

We all understand how our work is affected by those in authority over us—whether our manager is kind and capable or condescending and critical. As Christians, no matter whom we work for, ultimately we serve the perfect boss. Our aim in this life is to be pleasing to Him no matter what our occupation. When we view our earthly employment through a heavenly lens, it gives meaning to the most menial jobs and motivation for the most difficult.

A TREASURE CHEST OF LAZY TRUTHS

Proverbs 26:13-16 paints a portrait of the sluggard that is hard to forget. Consider the following four characteristics of the lazy man: He doesn't work hard except to make excuses (verse 13); he sleeps all the time but can't find any rest (verse 14); he never does anything yet he's tired all the time (verse 15); and he lives like a fool but he thinks he's the smartest guy around (verse 16). Let's look at each of these characteristics for just a moment.

First, we see that the sluggard works hard only when it comes to thinking up reasons for not working at all. Verse 13 gives an example of his elaborate excuses: "The sluggard says, 'There is a lion in the road! A lion is in the open square!'" A parallel verse in Proverbs 22:13 repeats this same story: "The sluggard says, 'There is a lion outside; I will be killed in the streets!'" In order to avoid work, the lazy man invents the most creative and ridiculous reasons not to leave his house. Sure he would love to get a job, but how can he? What if he were to end up in a car accident? What if a fire, an earthquake, or a tornado were to come along? He would have shown up for his interview but his car broke down, the bus was late, his cell phone died, or something else came up. Excuses, excuses, excuses. He is totally irresponsible and unreliable, yet he always has an answer for why it isn't his fault. And his reasons tend to get more and more outlandish. "Look! I think I see a lion!" he cries. "I should probably stay at home today. I'm allergic to lions."

In Proverbs 26:14 we see a second and rather ironic truth about the lazy man: Though he sleeps all the time, he never gets any rest. The verse reads, "As the door turns on its hinges, so does the sluggard on his bed." Back and forth, tossing and turning through the night, the sluggard never experiences anything more than an uneasy slumber. Perhaps it is because the weight of his unmet responsibilities is heavy upon him. He knows his resources are running thin, and that winter is coming and creditors will soon be knocking on his door. Perhaps it is simply the result of his apathy as he discovers that a life of listlessness quickly becomes boring and aimless. In either case, the man who hugs his pillow when he should be working will never find the peaceful rest he seeks. Though he does everything he can to maintain his supine position, there is no sound sleep for the sluggard. Instead of digging a trench and making an hourly wage he has produced a groove in his mattress on which he spends countless hours sleeping, or trying to. But at least he has no calluses and he won't get a sunburn.

Verse 15 gives us a third insight into his life: "The sluggard buries his hand in the dish; he is weary of bringing it to his mouth again." Although he never does any work, the lazy man feels tired all the time. He is too lethargic to even finish eating! Solomon's point is that sloth has a way of earning interest. Laziness breeds more laziness as the miserable state of the sluggard only gets worse over time. In this case, his condition has become so pitiful that even gravity is too laborious for him to overcome. About all he can do anymore is change the channel from one reality show to the next, watching other people live and work because he just doesn't have the energy.

Another irony is presented in verse 16: "The sluggard is wiser in his own eyes than seven men who can give a discreet answer." In spite of his deplorable state—as a bankrupt, homebound, languid, couch-sitting bum—the lazy man still thinks he is pretty smart. Perhaps that is why he refuses to listen to the wisdom he so desperately needs to hear. He thinks he knows better than everybody else. In his mind, even a roomful of scholars would have nothing to offer him. But in the end, his pride will result in an inevitable downfall. As Solomon stated just a few verses earlier, "Do you see a man wise in his own eyes? There is more hope for a fool than for him" (verse 12). What the sluggard cannot understand is the tremendous value in the completion of tasks. Alexander Maclaren provided this helpful counsel:

> No unwelcome tasks become any the less unwelcome by putting them off till tomorrow. It is only when they are behind us and done, that we begin to find that there is a sweetness to be tasted afterwards, and that the remembrance of unwelcome duties unhesitatingly done is welcome and pleasant. Accomplished, they are full of blessing, and there is a smile on their faces as they leave us. Undone, they stand threatening and disturbing our tranquility, and hindering our communion with God. If there be lying before you any bit of work from which you shrink, go straight up to it, and do it at once. The only way to get rid of it is to do it.[3]

This is the wisdom that the lazy man cannot comprehend. But those who are willing to work according to God's plan will experience the joy that comes from hard work and accomplishment.

LOOK, KIDS, A SLUGGARD!

In Proverbs 24:30-34, Solomon recounts a time he walked past the lazy man's farm. It was not a pretty picture:

> I passed by the field of the sluggard and by the vineyard of the man lacking sense, and behold, it was completely overgrown with thistles; its surface was covered with nettles, and its stone wall was broken down. When I saw, I reflected upon it; I looked, and received instruction. "A little sleep, a little slumber, a little folding of the hands to rest," then your poverty will come as a robber, and your want like an armed man.

The lazy man's life serves as an object lesson both for us and our children, teaching us that the fruit of fruitlessness is bitter and hard. Work is a public activity (cf. 1 Thessalonians 4:11-12), and those who work little and do it poorly bring a stigma on themselves. "Like vinegar to the teeth and smoke to the eyes, so is the lazy one to those who send him" (Proverbs 10:26). The slothful man's reputation is well deserved. His task list is unfinished, his property is run down, and his bank account is empty. By doing nothing, he has done all this to himself. What a motivational warning this is for us!

At this point, we might also consider a variant form of the lazy man—the lottery dreamer and pyramid schemer. This is the sluggard who thinks he can avoid work by getting rich quick through questionable means such as gambling and multilevel marketing scams. The book of Proverbs speaks to this man as well: "He who tills his land will have plenty of food, but he who follows empty pursuits will have poverty in plenty" (28:19). And elsewhere, "Wealth obtained by fraud dwindles, but the one who gathers by labor increases it" (13:11; cf. 20:17). The desire to make a quick buck, without putting forth any legitimate effort, is typical of the sluggard. Eleven times out of ten it backfires on him—and he finds himself with less than he had before. But even if he were to hit the jackpot, it wouldn't last. Those who don't work for their wealth seldom learn the real cost behind it. They are rightly described by the old truism "Easy come, easy go." Soon they find themselves back in their poverty with nothing to show for their earlier good fortune.

WHY WE WORK

Work is not ultimately about gaining wealth or finding fulfillment in your field. Rather, its fundamental purpose is to bring glory to God. This is the meaning behind the word *vocation*, which finds its root in the Latin word for *calling*. Men who view their jobs as a God-given calling, no matter what they do, connect their daily work with a higher purpose. God has given us the strength to provide for our families (1 Timothy 5:8), to honor Him in our attitudes (Ephesians 6:5-9), to show love for others (Mark 12:31), and to be a light to the world around us (Matthew 5:16). Work in any field takes on its intended meaning when men view their jobs as a calling from God. There is beauty in a job well done. Read what Proverbs 27:23–28:1 says:

> Know well the condition of your flocks, and pay attention to your herds; for riches are not forever, nor does a crown endure to all generations. When the grass disappears, the new growth is seen, and the herbs of the mountains are gathered in, the lambs will be for your clothing, and the goats will bring the price of a field, and there will be goats' milk enough for your food, for the food of your household, and sustenance for your maidens.

With poetic language the teacher extols the worth of work. He commends work that is done with precision and skill. He also reminds the faithful laborer that riches are not ultimate. They will pass away. Work doesn't exist so that workers can horde wealth for themselves. It exists so that a man can provide for his family and glorify God in both the process and the outcome. There is no quantifiable difference between the secular and the sacred when it comes to work. All honest work, done to the glory of Christ, is pleasing to God. Whether you work in construction or a coffee shop, in retail or in education, you are called to do your work to the glory of God.

In this chapter, our focus has been on the sluggard. But we would be remiss if we did not mention an equally dangerous (although very different) approach to work: the idolatry of the workaholic. Those who make a god out of their jobs, living for work while neglecting their other responsibilities and relationships, will likewise experience disastrous consequences. By contrast, the godly man finds the appropriate balance between the inaction of the sluggard and the obsession of the workaholic. We are called to work hard for God's glory. But we are never to make work an idol to the point that it becomes our focus to the exclusion of everything else.

As we've seen from the example of the sluggard, laziness leads to a hard life lived in opposition to God and His plan. To quote from the book of Proverbs one last time, "The way of the lazy is as a hedge of thorns, but the path of the upright is a highway" (15:19). Men of the Word understand that they were created by God to work hard. So with hearts of joy, they diligently serve their Lord and their families in their efforts to honor God and provide for their own.

Real Men Love Their Enemies
Lessons from the Life of Elisha

JESSE JOHNSON

M artin Seliane was an insurrectionist who thought he had justice on his side. In the early 1990s Martin was a leader in the African National Congress, the major black political party in South Africa. Violence was a tool he employed often in his battle against apartheid. He thought nothing of shooting his enemies, especially if they were helping to enforce the governmental system of racial segregation. At that point in his life, Martin hated whites. And for him, hatred was not a harmless emotion, but a feeling that erupted into hostile aggression.

Adriaan Vlok was South Africa's Minister of Law and Order, charged with enforcing apartheid. Specifically, he was tasked with finding and punishing people like Martin. To accomplish this he used hit squads, chemical weapons, and old-fashioned assassinations. He ordered the firebombing of theaters that showed anti-government films; and in the final years of apartheid he rounded up his opposition, many of whom were never seen again.

For some of us, an enemy is a neighbor who gossips, a co-worker who spreads lies, or a family member intent on destroying our reputation. For others, an enemy might be a competing business, an opponent in athletics, or a rival at work. But there are those who have enemies of a more serious nature. For example, soldiers at war do not have to guess who the enemy is. For Martin Seliane, his enemy was Adriaan Vlok.

THE EXAMPLE OF ELISHA

As we will see in this chapter, real men love their enemies. Perhaps no one in Israel's history had more opportunities to demonstrate that than the prophet Elisha.

Elisha was God's chosen messenger during particularly hostile times. His predecessor, Elijah, was run out of the country when Queen Jezebel tried to have him killed. In the face of this rejection, Elijah fled into the wilderness and begged for God to take his life. Instead, God gave him a final task: to anoint Elisha as his successor (1 Kings 19:16). Thus Elisha became a prophet with no shortage of enemies. He was hated by those who hated Elijah and Yahweh (including the king), opposed by those who served the false god Baal, and even ambushed by the armies that waged war against Israel. He was betrayed by his friends, doubted by his followers, and despised by nearly everyone else.

Yet he responded by consistently loving his enemies.

That is not to say Elisha was a total pacifist. In fact, when God first made Elisha a prophet, the Lord said that He would use Elisha to "put to death" the worshipers of Baal (1 Kings 19:17). At one point, when a mob of nearly 50 young men surrounded Elisha and peppered him with insults, God sent along two bears who mauled 42 of the mockers (2 Kings 2:23-24). While Elisha was with the Israelite army in a battle against Moab, he waited until God caused the Moabites to hallucinate, then he instructed the Israelites to strike them down (2 Kings 3). When God authorized its use, Elisha was not adverse to violence.

Still, the record of Elisha's life reflects that he personally showed a persistent love to his worst enemies. He chose Jericho—a city filled with the enemies of God—as the site of his first public miracle. Hundreds of years earlier, the Lord had declared that anyone who dared to settle there would be cursed (Joshua 6:26). Yet Elisha cleansed the land and purified the water, effectively ending the curse against this city (2 Kings 2:18-22; 4:38-44).

Syria was Israel's most dangerous and feared enemy. When Elisha was a teenager, the Syrians plundered the temple and kidnapped the royal family (1 Kings 20:2-3). When Israel joined forces with Judah to defend their shared border from Syrian incursion, the Syrians not only killed wicked King Ahab, but also the God-fearing king of Judah, Jehoshaphat.

But despite their national animosity, when the leader of the Syrian army contracted leprosy, he sought out Elisha. In fact, at the time Naaman came to Elisha, the Syrian army was preparing to attack Israel and besiege her capital city. That siege was so severe it forced the Israelites to resort to cannibalism in order to survive (2 Kings 6:24-31). And still, when Naaman came to the prophet for help, Elisha did not see a wicked general, but rather a man who was humbled by circumstances and ready to turn to God in faith. Elisha told his enemy how to be healed—essentially by trusting in the Lord—and Naaman believed. In fact, the Syrian general responded to his restored skin with a confession of faith that no northern king of Israel would ever make: "Behold now, I know that there is no God in all the earth, but in Israel" (2 Kings 5:15).

No single event crystallizes Elisha's love for his enemies as much as the attempt on his life described in 2 Kings 6. Because Elisha was aiding the Israelite military, the Syrian king ordered his men to ambush and kill Elisha. In the middle of the night, Elisha's house was surrounded by "horses and chariots and a great army" sent by the Syrians to assassinate him (2 Kings 6:14).

The prophet, unarmed yet unafraid, went out to meet his adversaries. They moved into position to attack but were struck with blindness by the Lord. Then they were supernaturally led to believe that Elisha was their leader. In an amazing turn of events, the would-be target escorted his blind assailants on a ten-mile journey deep into Israel. He took them straight to Israel's capital and brought them inside the city. When the gates closed behind them their eyes were opened, and the Syrian assassins realized that they had been taken captive.

The Israelite king reasonably wanted to slaughter his newly arrested enemies. But Elisha said, "You shall not kill them." Instead he commanded the king to "set bread and water before them, that they may eat and drink and go to their master" (2 Kings 6:22). Not content with merely giving them bread and water, Elisha saw to it that this captive band of his enemies was served "a great feast" (verse 23). In fact, Elisha himself personally prepared the meal for the men who had been trying to kill him just a few hours earlier.

LOVE IS AGAINST THE GRAIN

When we look to the New Testament, we see this same love for one's enemies expressed in the teachings of Christ and the apostles. Jesus' command to love your enemies is certainly one of the most countercultural of all biblical injunctions. Fallen human nature is proud and self-centered. It inevitably desires to be honored, loved, and respected. But an enemy is someone who actively opposes you, confronts you, taunts you, and even wishes to see you experience harm. Needless to say, it is instinctive to hate your enemies.

Yet Jesus taught His followers to "love [their] enemies" (Matthew 5:44; Luke 6:27). He commanded us to love those whom we are most inclined to oppose because they hate us and desire our downfall.

Love is active. It is an emotion that produces commitment, and it is intense. At its core, love wants the best for others. A husband loves his wife, so he wants her to enjoy physical protection, financial provision, and spiritual sustenance. A father loves his children, so he wants them to grow in every aspect of life and godliness. That is the essence of love. And that is the emotion the Bible commands Christians to have toward those who hate and persecute them.

We can be tempted to think that neutrality is an agreeable middle ground. We might think, *I won't wish for their harm, but I certainly won't wish for their blessing.* But God calls us to *love* our enemies. We are not to merely tolerate them or quietly hope they will go away. Instead, we are to love them. And that requires action.

The mandate to love our enemies may seem unfair and unreasonable. It feels like it is the opposite of justice, and it is drastically different than the way those in the world live. It runs contrary to human nature and our internal inclinations. Self-defense dictates that, at minimum, we flee from our enemies. But self-denial calls us to love them, because that is what Jesus commanded.

And here is the catch: We cannot just *say* we love our enemies. We have to *actually* love them. The Bible knows nothing of a half-hearted or reluctant love. Real biblical love demands that we mourn over our enemies' loss and rejoice at their gain. We want the best for our enemies because we love them with a love that is modeled by God. Indifference is not love because it is not like God, who actively loves His enemies.

HOW TO LOVE THE UNLOVABLE

Jesus did not leave us guessing about the practical implications of loving our enemies. In fact, He taught three concrete ways His followers should express affection toward those who oppose them.

First, Jesus told His disciples, "Pray for those who persecute you" (Matthew 5:44). An obvious way to express love is to prayerfully intercede for those who hate us. We can pray for their blessing and repentance; and we can pray that we will endure their opposition with patience and grace.

Prayer takes discipline. The prayer our Lord described is not a one-time passing request to God. It is a constant and persistent intercession that flows from a heart of love. Prayer is a practice, and it requires a sacrifice of time and thought. Intentionally striving to diligently pray for anyone is a discipline, and Jesus instructed us to apply that effort toward our enemies' good.

Second, Jesus commanded us to "do good to those who hate you" (Luke 6:27). A simple test to see if you really love your enemies is to ask yourself, "Do I want what is best for them?" Authentic love desires that benefit go to the person loved. But notice that we are not merely to *desire* their good, we are commanded to *participate* in doing good for them. If our enemy has a need, we are called to help meet it. Solomon said it this way: "If your enemy is hungry, give him food to eat; and if he is thirsty, give him water to drink" (Proverbs 25:21).

Our expressions of love should also include a desire for our enemies' spiritual good. After all, what could be better than wanting our enemies to be reconciled to God through faith in His Son? Beyond mere desire, we can be the means of evangelizing them. Providing food and water is good, but taking the time to patiently explain the gospel is even better. If our enemies respond in faith, then they will become our brothers and sisters in Christ. But if they respond by persecuting us, we can rejoice in knowing that our reward in heaven is great (Matthew 5:11-12). When we suffer with patient endurance, our lives serve as a powerful witness to the truth of the gospel (cf. 1 Peter 2:20). That is evangelistic love.

Third, Christ instructed His followers to "lend, expecting nothing in return" (Luke 6:35). Beyond doing good and praying for good, the Lord asks us to give to our enemies. When you lend to an enemy, you are essentially parting with whatever it is you have loaned. What kind of enemy returns borrowed items?

It's important to note that Jesus is speaking of a truth more profound than the simple fact that your enemy might steal from you.

Lending implies reciprocity. Our society understands this principle well. If we do a favor for someone else (such as lending that person something he or she needs), we usually expect to receive a favor in return. But that is not the attitude Jesus wants us to have with regard to our enemies. We are to lend to them without ever anticipating anything in return. That is the kind of sacrificial love to which Christ calls us. We are to want what is best for our enemies, and we are to actively pursue their good with the full knowledge that they probably won't return the favor.

MANLINESS, VIOLENCE, LOVE, AND PACIFISM

While the command to love one's enemies applies equally to both genders, there is a sense in which it has particularly masculine implications. Men are physically stronger than women, and husbands are the protectors of their wives. When nations go to war, historically it has been men who have sacrificed their lives for their country. It is correct to think of masculinity as encompassing strength, valor, and bravery. The willingness to stand for justice, to fight for the oppressed, and to lay down one's life for a greater principle is indeed part of being an honorable man. But courage is noble only when it is inextricably tied to a real love for one's enemies. Absent that affection, military-style manhood is barbaric, not biblical.

The stereotype of manliness as bravado is the polar opposite of the kind of love Jesus prescribed. Any culture that defines masculinity solely in terms of brute violence misses the biblical mark. True masculinity displays a genuine love for others. In our culture (even among evangelicals), it is frustrating to see manhood more closely associated with cage fighting than peacekeeping.

On the other hand, the call to love one's enemies is not a call to radical pacifism or complete nonviolence in every situation. Elisha's own example gives evidence to that fact. Under God's direction, Elisha put many followers of Baal to death (1 Kings 19:17).

Yet he also rebuked the king of Israel for refusing to show love to his enemies (2 Kings 6:22). How are we to reconcile the two? First, it should be obvious that nonviolence and love are not the same thing. Turning the other cheek may demonstrate self-control, but unless it flows from a heart of sincere affection, it falls short of God's standard.

Second, God has placed every man in a complex set of relationships—each of which has a different level of priority. We are part of the body of Christ. We have families, friends, and acquaintances. We are residents of a city and citizens of a country. The Bible commands us to serve the church, obey the government, and honor the king. Likewise, God demands that we love our wives, children, neighbors, and enemies.

Those commands have different applications and may occasionally come into conflict with each other. For example, if the government commands us to do something that contradicts the Bible, our obedience to God (our highest priority) trumps our allegiance to our country (a lower priority). Similarly, if a friend or family member is in physical danger, and we are in a position to defend that person, then the priority of our love for that individual guides our response to the enemy—even if that response requires physical force. If we must make a choice between protecting our family (a high priority) and showing love to our enemy (a lower priority), the decision is not difficult. To refuse to physically protect victims of violence is to refuse to love those people, and that kind of pacifism—in the name of loving your enemies—is ironically unloving.

The point is that real masculinity is defined neither by brute force nor complete nonviolence. That is why the Bible can command us to turn the other cheek while, at the same time, remind us that the government bears the sword to punish evildoers (Matthew 5:39; Romans 13:4). A mark of Christian maturity is the ability to show love to an enemy at great expense to oneself, while also understanding the responsibility one owes to his family and community.

WHEN AN ENEMY IS A NEIGHBOR

When the Syrians opened their eyes and discovered that they had been trapped by Elisha, they probably thought a quick death was the best they could hope for. The Israelite king was understandably eager to accommodate their wish. Elisha's intervention on their behalf is remarkable because of the insight that it shows.

Elisha stopped the king's plan by reminding him that the law says, in essence, God's people are to love their enemies. Actually, the law says that God's people are to love their neighbors (Leviticus 19:18). The Pharisees of Jesus' day (nearly 700 years after Elisha) took that to mean: "Great! I'll love my neighbor, and hate my enemy." But Elisha told the king that by taking his enemies into his city, the king had made them his neighbors.

Hence the Pharisees, who surely knew the story of Elisha, should not have been surprised at Jesus' words in the Sermon on the Mount (Matthew 5:44). Jesus spoke to a truth realized by Elisha but forgotten by the self-righteous. If someone is consistently opposing you, they become your neighbor by nature of their close proximity to you. Thus, one of the reasons you are to love your enemy is because he *is* your neighbor.

Most likely our enemies are not strangers, but people in our family, church, or workplace. Elisha was opposed more by the Israelites than by the Syrians. In fact, the Israelite king who watched Elisha feed the Syrians then ordered the prophet to be beheaded (2 Kings 6:31). The Israelites rejected Elisha because they had rebelled against his God, and that is the way it always works. When people reject the Lord, they inevitably oppose those who belong to Him.

WHY WE LOVE THE UNLOVABLE

God's Word gives two surprising reasons why we are to love our enemies. First, *God is love*. Christians are told to "be imitators of God" (Ephesians 5:1). In the context of Ephesians 4 and 5, that command refers to forgiving those who have offended us. Such certainly applies to loving our enemies.

God has numerous enemies. The world is filled with people who are alienated from Him. Even we who are believers were formerly hostile to the truth (Romans 5:10). Nevertheless, God is the example of how to love an enemy. When we were still at enmity with Him, Christ died for us.

Sinners deserve immediate hell. Yet God patiently allows them to enjoy life—giving them time to repent even though most never do. One obvious example of God's common grace toward unrighteous men is rain. When the rain comes, it falls not only on those who love God, but also on those who have rebelled against Him. The sun, likewise, shines on both the just and the unjust.

Jesus pointed to the sun and the rain as demonstrating God's love for His enemies. He said, "Love your enemies...so that you may be sons of your Father who is in heaven; for He causes His sun to rise on the evil and the good, and sends rain on the righteous and the unrighteous" (Matthew 5:45). If God can extend patience and kindness toward His enemies, then we should love our enemies too.

A second reason we can love our enemies is because *God is sovereign*. That may not be an easy truth to appreciate, but the fact is that God gave us our enemies. They did not just appear; rather, they exist under the authority and sovereign purposes of God. He rules the world, and nothing happens outside of His prescription or permission. Our enemies often sin against us, and they will be judged for their actions. At the same time, it is always good to remember that they are under God's ultimate authority.

The reality is that, like everything in life, God uses our enemies both for our good and His glory (Romans 8:28). A clear example of this truth is found in 2 Corinthians 12, where Paul begged God to take away his "thorn in the flesh" (verse 7). The context makes it clear that this "thorn" was a person who opposed Paul's ministry—likely a false teacher attempting to undermine the apostle. Though Paul asked three times for the thorn to be removed, he was told that he must endure the suffering and learn to depend fully on God's grace (verse 9). Paul's enemy was an instrument used by God for his sanctification. It is easier to love our enemies when we understand that they were sent by the Lord for our good and His glory.

THE POWER OF RECONCILIATION

We began this chapter with the story of Martin Seliane and Adriaan Vlok.

When apartheid ended in 1994, Adriaan Vlok's wife committed suicide. The former Minister of Law and Order was watching his life fall apart and was almost certainly going to be tried for atrocities committed under his watch. His desperation drove him to a Christian church, where he gave his life to Jesus Christ. Adriaan then sought out his former enemies, many of whom had barely survived his earlier attempts to kill them, and he repented. He often publicly washed the feet of the people whom, just a few years before, he had tried to kill.

Meanwhile, Martin Seliane (the former leader within the ANC) attended a meeting put on by Campus Crusade. After watching the *Jesus* film, he also became a Christian. He fell in love with the Bible's power to transform lives, attended seminary, and went on to pastor a church in one of the poorest parts of South Africa. When he heard in the local news that Adriaan—his former enemy—had become a Christian, he invited him to share the pulpit at his church.

His invitation produced one of the most memorable scenes of postapartheid South Africa. The former enforcer of racial segregation came into a squatter village to preach at the church of a former enemy. Twenty years earlier either man would have killed the other, but now—in Christ—the two men stood together as a vivid example of what it means to love your enemy.

In all of their past fighting and killing, these men embodied their culture's understanding of masculinity. But as new creatures in Christ possessing supernatural love for each other, they exhibited a profound biblical truth: *Real men love their enemies.*

Real Men Share the Gospel

Lessons from the Book of Acts

KEVIN EDWARDS

Every true Christian wants to share the gospel with others. But too often we don't do what we wish we would. For one reason or another, we allow less important things to crowd out that which is most important to God. Sharing the good news with others is one of the greatest responsibilities we have been given. Yet for many believers, it is frequently eclipsed by other activities that seem more urgent or fun. The goal of this chapter is to help you move from sitting on the sidelines as a fan of evangelism to getting on the field as an active participant. As we look to the example of Jesus and the apostles, we are quickly reminded of a key characteristic of Christian manhood: *Real men share the gospel.*

To understand how important this is to God, let's start by looking at what Jesus Himself said about what it means to truly follow Him.

JESUS CHRIST—THE PERFECT GOSPEL WITNESS

When Jesus revealed His identity as the Son of God to His

disciples, He quickly had to correct their expectations. They were looking for a Messiah who would swoop down from heaven, eliminate the Roman invaders who ruled over Israel, and instantly bring in the Old Testament blessings God had promised His people (Ephesians 3:12-20).

But Jesus' disciples did not understand that before the glory of the Messianic kingdom could come, the Messiah had to suffer (Isaiah 53:1-12). So the Lord had to tell them what it was going to cost Him to be their Savior: "He began to teach them that the Son of Man must suffer many things and be rejected by the elders and the chief priests and the scribes, and be killed, and after three days rise again" (Mark 8:31; cf. Matthew 16:21). As Jesus explained to them, His path to eternal glory went through the cross.

In depicting His own suffering, the Lord defined the cost of being His disciple: "If anyone wishes to come after Me, he must deny himself, and take up his cross and follow Me" (Matthew 16:24). To follow Jesus begins with self-denial, replacing all selfish desires for sin with a singular passion to obey and follow Him—no matter where that leads. A true disciple is willing to take up a cross—to start on a death march and suffer humiliation, pain, and even martyrdom.

To come to Jesus Christ for salvation is not to raise a hand or sign a card, although such things may sometimes be done at the time of repentance. To come to Him is to come to the end of one's self and one's sin, and to become so desirous for Christ and His righteousness that one is willing to make any sacrifice to follow Him. That kind of commitment characterizes genuine disciples, and it includes a willingness to tell others about the Savior. They are even willing to die, if necessary, to take the gospel to the lost.

But many Christians do not live like that, let alone evangelize like that. Too many believers think being a witness consists of telling people that they can have a better, easier life by embracing Jesus. But that was not the message Jesus taught His disciples, nor was it the message they took to the world.

THE GOSPEL JESUS PREACHED

Jesus' message was not the easy-believism or health-and-wealth message we hear so often today. When the Lord began His public ministry here on earth, He "began to preach and say, 'Repent, for the kingdom of heaven is at hand'" (Matthew 4:17). Elsewhere, we read that He was "preaching the gospel of God, and saying, 'The time is fulfilled, and the kingdom of God is at hand; repent and believe in the gospel'" (Mark 1:14-15). Jesus told the Pharisees, "I have not come to call the righteous but sinners to repentance" (Luke 5:32). The gospel that Jesus proclaimed began with a mandate to repent.

Repentance from sin was at the core of Jesus' message. He began His earthly ministry by demanding repentance, and in His closing charge to His disciples He commanded them to preach repentance (Luke 24:47). But what exactly does it mean *to repent*? When a sinner repents, He makes a complete turn away from sin and whole-heartedly looks to God in humble, obedient faith. John the Baptist preached this gospel (Matthew 3:2) prior to Jesus' public ministry, And the apostles taught it as well.

A helpful description of repentance is found in 2 Corinthians 7:10-11. There, the apostle Paul wrote:

> The sorrow that is according to the will of God produces a repentance without regret, leading to salvation, but the sorrow of the world produces death. For behold what earnestness this very thing, this godly sorrow, has produced in you: what vindication of yourselves, what indignation, what fear, what longing, what zeal, what avenging of wrong!

Worldly sorrow can produce an emotional response caused by feelings of shame, guilt, and even remorse. But godly sorrow is categorically different because it results in real and lasting repentance.

Godly sorrow is a genuine sorrow over sin. It causes the offender to eagerly pursue what is right, to genuinely run from his wrongdoing, to prove his true repentance to others, and to hate the wickedness he formerly loved. It resolves not to dishonor the Savior again, commits to restoring broken relationships, seeks to make things right, and determines to walk in holiness.

When Jesus called people to repent, those who truly turned from sin had an immediate God-given desire to fight for purity in every aspect of life. They were no longer slaves of sin, but slaves of Christ—and that transformation was evident in how they lived. After Jesus' death and resurrection, the disciples were commissioned by Him to "go…and make disciples of all the nations" (Matthew 28:19). As apostles sent by Christ to spread the good news, they preached the same message of repentance that Jesus had.

THE APOSTLES' PREACHING:
A MESSAGE OF REPENTANCE

The first sermon in the book of Acts, preached by Peter on the day of Pentecost, was an unmistakable message of repentance. Peter spoke to thousands of people in Jerusalem, powerfully explaining to them that the One whom they had crucified was in fact the Messiah, their Lord and Savior. "When they heard this, they were pierced to the heart, and said to Peter and the rest of the apostles, 'Brethren, what shall we do?' Peter said to them, 'Repent, and each of you be baptized in the name of Jesus Christ for the forgiveness of your sins; and you will receive the gift of the Holy Spirit'" (Acts 2:37-38). On that day 3000 people turned to follow Christ.

The second sermon Peter preached followed the miraculous healing of a crippled beggar at the temple (Acts 3). As crowds rushed forward in amazement, Peter made it clear that the power to heal this lame man did not come from him but from God, who by His power had also raised Jesus from the dead. Peter called the people to respond to God and "repent and return, so that your sins may be wiped away" (Acts 3:19).

Peter's message did not change when the spiritual leaders of Israel imprisoned him and the other apostles, demanding that they stop telling people about Christ. After being miraculously released from jail and returning to the Temple to preach, Peter and the apostles explained to the spiritual leaders why they could not stop proclaiming the gospel:

> We must obey God rather than men. The God of our fathers raised up Jesus, whom you had put to death by hanging Him on a cross. He is the one whom God exalted to His right hand as a Prince and a Savior, to grant repentance to Israel, and forgiveness of sins. And we are witnesses of these things; and so is the Holy Spirit, whom God has given to those who obey Him (Acts 5:29-32).

The call to repentance was not well received by the religious leaders. The apostles were almost put to death (verse 33), but instead were beaten and released (verse 40). Even in the face of suffering and possible martyrdom, they dutifully preached the message of repentance.

Another example of that apostolic emphasis is found in Acts 17. Paul was provoked by the rampant idolatry of the people of Athens, so he proclaimed to them that "having overlooked the times of ignorance, God is now declaring to men that *all people everywhere should repent*, because He has fixed a day in which He will judge the world in righteousness through a Man whom He has appointed, having furnished proof to all men by raising Him from the dead" (verses 30-31, emphasis added). Later, when he stood on trial before Agrippa, Paul reiterated the fact that the message of repentance was central to his evangelistic mission. He told the king, "I did not prove disobedient to the heavenly vision, but kept declaring both to those of Damascus first, and also at Jerusalem and then throughout all the region of Judea, and even to the Gentiles, that they should repent and turn to God, performing deeds appropriate to repentance" (Acts 26:19-20).

The gospel message that the apostles preached always called sinners to repent and embrace Christ. They were faithful to preach the gospel as they had received it from Jesus. And we must do the same. Sadly, the church today has watered down the gospel message, often removing any emphasis on sin and the need to repent from it. But the true gospel—the one Jesus and the apostles preached, and the one that we should preach—requires both genuine faith and heartfelt repentance, a sincere willingness to turn from sin and follow Christ.

THE APOSTLES' PERSPECTIVE:
A LIFE OF SACRIFICE

The apostles got the gospel right. They also demonstrated a courageous willingness to suffer for the truth. They faithfully denied themselves, took up their crosses daily, and followed Christ. Their sacrifice for the gospel meant going to unfamiliar cultures, maintaining an unwavering commitment, and paying unknown costs.

Unfamiliar Cultures

When Jesus gave His parting charge to the apostles, He emphasized that the gospel was to be proclaimed in "all the nations" (Matthew 28:19). The apostles were to take the gospel to people they did not know and into cultures that were foreign to them. The Lord instructed them, "You will receive power when the Holy Spirit has come upon you; and you shall be My witnesses both in Jerusalem, and in all Judea and Samaria, and even to the remotest part of the earth" (Acts 1:8). Here we find the outline for the rest of the book of Acts—God's strategy for the expansion of the gospel.

Throughout Acts, we see how God executed that plan, beginning in Jerusalem with Peter and Stephen, continuing into the rest of Judea and neighboring Samaria with Philip and Peter, and eventually spreading all the way to Rome with Paul. Initially, the expansion of the gospel beyond Israel was not easy for Peter and the other apostles to understand. Peter had to be shown, through a vision, that "God is not one to show partiality, but in every nation the man who fears Him and does what is right is welcome to Him" (Acts 10:34-35).

The principle here for us is that we are responsible, with God's help, to take the gospel beyond our family, our neighborhood, and our city. This requires sacrifice and a willingness to put ourselves into situations where we can meet unbelievers, even if their cultural background is unfamiliar to us. God intends the gospel to go to people of all nations. To be a disciple of Christ is to be actively involved in missions, both across the street and around the world.

Unwavering Commitment

With undying courage, the apostles repeatedly endured intense persecution and hardship for the advance of the gospel. They were committed to obeying the Great Commission no matter what the consequences. In fact, the apostle Paul suffered greatly for that commitment. In 2 Corinthians 11:21-30, he outlined some of the ways he had suffered for the gospel—including labors and journeys, imprisonments and beatings, shipwrecks and sleeplessness, starvation and the constant threat of death. He faced "dangers from rivers, dangers from robbers, dangers from [his] countrymen, dangers from the Gentiles, dangers in the city, dangers in the wilderness, dangers on the sea, [and] dangers among false brethren" (verse 26).

Significantly, Paul wrote 2 Corinthians around AD 55, during his third missionary journey (cf. Acts 20:2-3). But the narrative in Acts, up to that point, mentions only one time that Paul was beaten (in Philippi, Acts 16:22), one imprisonment (also in Philippi, Acts 16:23), and one near-death stoning (in Lystra, Acts 14:19). Incredibly, only a small portion of the apostle's many sufferings are recorded in the book of Acts. Paul was clearly a man who suffered greatly for the gospel, and his commitment never wavered.

Paul faced many dangers and endured much suffering, and God honored his resolve and advanced the gospel through him. The bold apostle was not a glutton for punishment, intentionally placing himself in dangerous situations just so he could say he had suffered. But he was willing to suffer if that's what being faithful required. A true disciple is ready to do whatever it takes to spread the good news, and he is confident that God will help him remain obedient even in the midst of severe difficulty.

Paul's sacrificial commitment to preaching the gospel meant he did more than just plant the seed and walk away. When unbelievers responded to his message, he made sure they were grounded in the faith and connected to the local church before he moved on to the next city. He was careful to appoint godly leaders in the churches he planted—so that each congregation would survive after he left. At times he spent prolonged periods in certain cities (such as Corinth and Ephesus) to train and encourage the Christians in those places. In his absence he wrote letters to the churches, continually encouraging them to remain true to the Savior. Paul was deeply committed to the believers' sanctification even when he was away from them. As the Great Commission makes clear, the goal of evangelism is not just to produce *converts*, but to make *disciples*. Being a faithful witness requires that we be ready to sacrificially commit our time and energy to those who respond to the gospel—teaching them sound doctrine and helping them grow in Christlikeness.

UNKNOWN COST

When the church in Jerusalem began to grow, the apostles continually devoted themselves "to prayer and to the ministry of the word" so they could accomplish the task that the Lord had given them—the task to "make disciples" (Acts 6:4; Matthew 28:19). God blessed the church and "the disciples were increasing in number"

(Acts 6:1). As more people repented and believed in Christ, the number of believers increased. More leaders were needed to shepherd the new converts and to teach them the Word of the Lord. One of those leaders was Stephen.

Stephen was a man of the Word. Luke, the author of Acts, said that Stephen was "a man full of faith and of the Holy Spirit" (Acts 6:5). He was chosen as one of seven "men of good reputation, full of the Spirit and of wisdom," to be in charge of the physical needs of the church in Jerusalem (Acts 6:3). One of the few details in the Bible regarding Stephen's ministry in the church was that he performed "great wonders and signs among the people" (Acts 6:8). And Stephen is one of very few men in history to have given a sermon that was recorded in its entirety in the Bible (in Acts 7). He is also the first-mentioned martyr of the church. That Stephen's listeners responded to his message by putting him to death shows us that we must be ready to suffer any cost in our proclamation of gospel.

Stephen's sermon, given in response to false accusations made against him by the religious leaders of Israel, was completely gospel-centered. He preached about the history of the nation from the days of Abraham until the building of the temple by King Solomon. By reviewing the repeated disobedience of the people, Stephen demonstrated that they had always rejected God's instruction, whether it came from Moses, the prophets, the priests, or the Son of God Himself. When the long-awaited Messiah came and preached repentance and salvation from sin, the people once again rebelled against God—and they put the Savior to death.

Being confronted in this way was more than Stephen's audience could take. At the end of the sermon, the religious leaders stoned him to death. But before he died, Stephen prayed, "Lord, do not hold this sin against them!" (Acts 7:60). With his dying breath he interceded for his murderers, echoing Christ's prayer on the cross for those who crucified Him. Stephen paid the highest price one could possibly pay for preaching the gospel. It cost him his life.

THE APOSTLES' POWER:
A RELIANCE ON THE SPIRIT

The level of sacrifice exhibited by the apostles was clearly beyond anything they could do in their own strength. And the response to the gospel—an invitation to give up everything and follow a crucified Messiah—was far greater than anyone could expect, humanly speaking. So where did the valor to preach the gospel come from? And where did the conviction to repent and believe that message come from?

Before Jesus returned to heaven, He bookended the Great Commission with two incredible truths. He told His followers, "*All authority has been given to Me in heaven and on earth.* Go therefore and make disciples of all the nations, baptizing them in the name of the Father and the Son and the Holy Spirit, teaching them to observe all that I commanded you; *and lo, I am with you always, even to the end of the age*" (Matthew 28:18-20, emphasis added).

The Lord did not leave His disciples alone to accomplish the mammoth task to which He called them. Rather, He reminded them of His absolute sovereign authority and never-ending presence with them. He would empower them to fulfill their mission. In Acts 1:8, Jesus told the apostles, "You will receive power when the Holy Spirit has come upon you, and you shall be My witnesses both in Jerusalem and in all Judea and Samaria, and even to the remotest part of the earth." The disciples had already witnessed the power of the Holy Spirit in salvation and through the miracles of Jesus. But now they were promised a new dimension of power, one which they received when they were filled by the Holy Spirit at Pentecost.

The power of the Spirit in the preaching of the gospel is highlighted throughout the book of Acts (cf. 2:47; 6:7; 9:31; 12:24; 16:5; 19:20; 28:30-31). Though the book is titled "The Acts of the Apostles," it is really "The Acts of the Holy Spirit as He Empowered the Apostles." In spite of seemingly insurmountable odds, the gospel went forth in power and thousands responded in repentant faith. If this had been merely a human effort, it certainly would have failed. The apostles would have thrown in the towel, and the saints would have given up. But the presence and power of God ensured that His work would not be overcome—and it will continue to expand until He returns.

That reality changed everything for the apostles. It should for us too. As faithful witnesses to the gospel, we can rest in the fact that our labor and sacrifice is empowered by God Himself. Nothing can stop Him or His plan. In proclaiming His truth, we can do anything He requires of us, no matter what the cost, because He is our strength and our ever-present Savior. Armed with that truth, as godly men, may we be found faithful to fulfill His calling by proclaiming His gospel.

Real Men Love the Church
Lessons from the Life of Paul

BRENT SMALL

D o you love the church? If you are a Christian, the answer should be an overwhelming "Yes!" But a growing number of evangelical men are not so sure. Just visit your local Christian bookstore and you'll find titles like *Why Men Hate Going to Church* and *Wild at Heart: Discovering the Secret of a Man's Soul*. Based on recent statistics, which show that more than 60 percent of regular church attendees are women, books like these are asking the obvious question: Where are all the men? Clearly, something is wrong.

Unfortunately, many such books—after correctly identifying a problem—offer solutions that are off-base. Some suggest that churches should be completely restructured to appeal to men, even if the end result looks nothing like the biblical paradigm for a church. Others are more extreme, encouraging men to ditch weekly worship services altogether and instead participate in more "masculine" activities such as mountain biking or camping in the woods. But those kinds of solutions always end in spiritual disaster. In reality, the only right response is to call Christian men to embrace the church as God commands them to do. If a man has no love for the body of Christ, the problem is not with the church, but with him.

To be sure, no local church is perfect. Even so, that is no excuse to avoid or neglect it. Consider the words of Charles Spurgeon, the famed British preacher of a century ago:

> Give yourself to the Church. You that are members of the Church have not found it perfect and I hope that you feel almost glad that you have not. If I had never joined a Church till I had found one that was perfect, I would never have joined one at all! And the moment I did join it, if I had found one, I should have spoiled it, for it would not have been a perfect Church after I had become a member of it. Still, imperfect as it is, it is the dearest place on earth to us…All who have first given themselves to the Lord, should, as speedily as possible, also give themselves to the Lord's people. How else is there to be a Church on the earth? If it is right for anyone to refrain from membership in the Church, it is right for everyone, and then the testimony for God would be lost to the world!
>
> As I have already said, the Church is faulty, but that is no excuse for you not joining it, if you are the Lord's. Nor need your own faults keep you back, for the Church is not an institution for perfect people, but a sanctuary for sinners saved by Grace, who, though they are saved, are still sinners and need all the help they can derive from the sympathy and guidance of their fellow believers. The Church is the nursery for God's weak children where they are nourished and grow strong. It is the fold for Christ's sheep—the home for Christ's family.[1]

Real men love the church in spite of its flaws. They do so primarily because they love the Lord, and the church is His bride. It is the place where His Word is preached, where His praise is sung, and where His people gather. To join with the saints each Sunday should be the Christian's highest joy. Those who struggle with boredom or indifference when it comes to the church would do well to heed Paul's sober advice in 2 Corinthians 13:5: "Test yourselves to see if you are in the faith."

But for those of us who belong to Christ, the church is the dearest place on earth. It is a profound delight even to be there. Thus, in whatever congregation God has placed us, we must become, as one of my seminary professors used to say, "churchmen"—men who are zealous to see the local body grow in Christlikeness and bring glory to God.

In this chapter, we will consider the example of one of the greatest churchmen who ever lived, the apostle Paul.

A MAN WHO LOVED THE CHURCH

It is almost an understatement to say that Paul loved the church. He prayed for, wept for, labored for, and literally bled for the church. Over the course of his missionary career, the tireless apostle planted, visited, instructed, rebuked, restored, and revisited numerous congregations of believers. The church consumed his life because, as Paul himself explained, "For to me, to live is Christ" (Philippians 1:21), and serving the Lord meant serving His body.

Paul's passion for the church was evident from the very beginning of his missionary work. As he and Barnabas traveled through the cities of Iconium and Lystra during their first missionary journey, they encountered intense persecution. So much so that while in Lystra, Paul was stoned by an angry crowd until presumed dead. Undeterred, Paul stood up and courageously went back into the city. The next day he and Barnabas traveled to Derbe, where they preached the gospel and saw many more souls won to Christ.

Derbe was the last stop on their journey. But Paul was not ready to quit. He and Barnabas decided to go home the same way they had come—back through the cities where they had just been violently mistreated. *Why?* Luke recorded the answer in Acts 14:21-23. Speaking of Derbe, he wrote:

> After they had preached the gospel to that city and had made many disciples, they returned to Lystra and to Iconium and to Antioch, strengthening the souls of the disciples, encouraging them to continue in the faith, and saying, "Through many tribulations we must enter the kingdom of God." When they had appointed elders for them in every church, having prayed with fasting, they commended them to the Lord in whom they had believed.

Paul and Barnabas traveled right back into harm's way because they were more concerned about the churches they had planted than their own physical safety. According to the Acts account, the missionaries worked to accomplish four very specific purposes: (1) to strengthen the souls of those who had believed; (2) to encourage the believers to remain steadfast in the faith; (3) to exhort them to persevere, knowing that they would endure many trials before they enter the kingdom of God; and (4) to establish leaders in those churches who could shepherd the people after Paul and Barnabas were gone. Paul and Barnabas willingly put their lives at risk to make sure each congregation was fully established and growing in the Word.

THE MOTIVATING
FACTORS BEHIND PAUL'S LOVE

What was it that motivated Paul's intense and courageous love for the church? What kept the apostle going even when he was physically assaulted by violent mobs or verbally attacked by false teachers? Let's consider three key motivating factors that fueled Paul's love for the body of Christ. These same factors should ignite a similar passion within our hearts.

Motivation 1: The Love of the Savior

First and foremost, Paul's love for the church flowed from his understanding and experience of Christ's love for him. Before his conversion, Paul was an enemy of the church. In Galatians 1:13, he described his unconverted state: "You have heard of my former manner of life in Judaism, how I used to persecute the church of God beyond measure and tried to destroy it." But the former persecutor soon became one of the church's greatest promoters. Upon his conversion and baptism he *immediately* began to proclaim Jesus in the synagogues, saying, "He is the Son of God" (Acts 9:20). The Savior's love for Paul, a love that had forgiven his sins and ushered him into a saving relationship with God, placed a forceful motivation in his heart. Once Paul experienced the love of Christ, he was changed forever.

In 2 Corinthians 5:14-15, Paul explained the compelling nature of Christ's love for him. He wrote, "The love of Christ controls us, having concluded this, that one died for all, therefore all died; and He died for all, so that they who live might no longer live for themselves, but for Him who died and rose again on their behalf." Paul was no longer controlled by his own desires, but by the love of Christ. The word Paul used for "controls" referred to the kind of dominance exhibited by an army general or a prison warden. Like a soldier under orders or even a prisoner behind bars, the apostle was enclosed, hemmed in and dominated by Christ's love. That governing reality moved him to live for the Lord and not himself.

The controlling influence of Christ's love is evident in Paul's mandate to preach the gospel. In 1 Corinthians 9:16 he explained, "I am under compulsion, for woe is me if I do not preach the gospel." Paul allowed no hardship to deter him from obeying that command and edifying the saints. In 1 Thessalonians 2:2 he wrote, "After we had already suffered and been mistreated in Philippi, as you know, we had the boldness in our God to speak to you the gospel of God amid much opposition." Such is the heart of a man who was dominated by the love of Christ, and subsequently committed to the church.

The implications of Paul's example are profound for us as Christian men. Like Paul, real men love the church because Christ loved it and gave His life for it. Real men are committed to God's people because His love now dominates their life—enabling them to die to themselves, live for the Lord, and selflessly serve others. As we consider Paul's example, we must ask ourselves, "Do I love the church? Or has my love grown cold?" If it has, the sole solution is to look to Christ in humble repentance. Only by rekindling our passion for Him can we recapture our love for His bride.

Motivation 2: The Needs of the Saints

A second reason Paul loved the church was that he loved those who make up the church—the saints. His greatest joy on earth was to be with the people of God, teaching and encouraging them. He delighted in serving them by meeting their spiritual needs, even when it meant great personal cost to himself.

Paul's pattern in the New Testament was to travel, proclaim the gospel, and plant churches. He occasionally stayed in one church for a number of months such as at Corinth, but his usual approach was to move from city to city. Along with Timothy, Titus, and others, Paul was very purposeful about establishing elders in each church to provide oversight and protection. This was rigorous work involving many physical hardships and constant dangers. And once Paul left a city, *the church there never left his mind.* In 2 Corinthians 11:23-28, Paul listed some of the difficulties he faced in his missionary travels:

> In far more labors, in far more imprisonments, [I have been] beaten times without number, often in danger of death. Five times I received from the Jews thirty-nine lashes. Three times I was beaten with rods, once I was stoned, three times I was shipwrecked, a night and a day I have spent in the deep. I have been on frequent

journeys, in dangers from rivers, dangers from robbers, dangers from my countrymen, dangers from the Gentiles, dangers in the city, dangers in the wilderness, dangers on the sea, dangers among false brethren; I have been in labor and hardship, through many sleepless nights, in hunger and thirst, often without food, in cold and exposure. Apart from such external things, *there is the daily pressure on me of concern for all the churches* (emphasis added).

What an amazing list! Let's be honest. After being stoned, beaten, shipwrecked, and facing a life full of dangers, most of us would be ready to quit. But not Paul. Not only did he endure all of those hardships, but something even greater remained a daily pressure on his mind: his concern for all the churches. His love for the saints weighed more heavily on him than anything else.

In 2 Corinthians 11:29, we get another remarkable glimpse into the apostle's heart. He wrote, "Who is weak without my being weak? Who is led into sin without my intense concern?" In 1 Corinthians 12:26 he similarly stated, "If one member suffers, all the members suffer with it; if one member is honored, all the members rejoice with it." Incredibly, Paul was personally invested in the spiritual well-being of every believer under his shepherding care. If another believer was weak, then he felt weak too.

Paul's first letter to the Thessalonians again demonstrates his intense love for the saints. Even though he was no longer in Thessalonica, he still eagerly longed to see them (2:17). They had come under many afflictions and Paul was concerned that their faith might fail. He desperately wanted to encourage them in person. But because he could not go himself, he sent Timothy to make sure they were standing firm. Even after Timothy brought back a good report, the burdened apostle still desired to visit them so as to "complete" whatever might be lacking in their faith (3:10). As was the case for all the churches Paul had planted, he loved the Thessalonians deeply. He continued to care about each church even after he was no longer present with the people.

Yet even Paul's absence did not keep him from doing his pastoral work. Separation from the churches drove the apostle to a higher source of sustaining power, none other than the Lord Himself. When Paul could not visit a church in person, he relieved his concern by praying for the people there. His words in Philippians 4:6-7 must have been a constant reminder to him not to worry about the ones he loved. Though there were contentions within the Philippian congregation (Philippians 4:2-3), the apostle comforted his readers and himself with these words: "Be anxious for nothing, but in everything by prayer and supplication with thanksgiving let your requests be made known to God. And the peace of God, which surpasses all comprehension, will guard your hearts and your minds in Christ Jesus." Continual and fervent prayer for the churches was Paul's primary way of loving them while he was away from them (cf. Romans 1:9; Ephesians 1:17). The intensity of his intercession reflected the depth of his affection.

Paul's love for the church placed a consuming demand on his life. Even in the midst of life-threatening circumstances, trials, and afflictions, Paul carried the daily pressure and burden of the churches on his shoulders. He wrote to them from prison. He was personally invested in their spiritual welfare and growth. He continually prayed on their behalf that they might grow in the knowledge of Christ. His life was consumed with the churches because he loved the people in them, warts and all. What a convicting example that is for us!

Motivation 3: The Identity of the Church

A third motivation we see evidenced in Paul's ministry is that he loved the church because he understood its unique identity as God's very own possession. Writing to Timothy, his son in the faith, Paul said, "I write so that you will know how one ought to conduct himself in the household of God, which is the church of the living

God, the pillar and support of the truth" (1 Timothy 3:15). The apostle's description makes it clear that the church is not like any other institution on earth. It is unique, being built by Christ Himself (Matthew 16:18). It is *the church of the living God*, and that sets it completely apart from anything else on earth.

Other New Testament passages similarly identify the church as the Lord's possession. It is variously described as Christ's body (Ephesians 1:22-23), Christ's bride (Revelation 21:9), God's flock (1 Peter 5:2), God's field (1 Corinthians 3:9), God's temple (1 Corinthians 3:16-17), and God's household (Ephesians 2:19). Quite clearly, it belongs to Him. In Acts 20:28, Paul referred to it as "the church of God which He purchased with His own blood"—that is, with the blood of His Son Jesus Christ. God redeemed it "not...with perishable things like silver or gold...but with precious blood, as of a lamb unblemished and spotless, the blood of Christ" (1 Peter 1:18-19). In fact, the Lord saved every believer to "purify for Himself a people for His own possession, zealous for good deeds" (Titus 2:14). As 1 Peter 2:9 declares, the church consists of "a people for [God's] own possession, that [they] may proclaim the excellencies of him who called [them] out of darkness into his marvelous light" (ESV).

In the New Testament, the Greek word usually translated "church" is the word *ekklesia*. It carries the idea of "the called ones"—those who were called out of the world, redeemed by Jesus' blood, and brought into fellowship with Him and His followers. In a general sense, the term *ekklesia* applies to all believers everywhere, the universal church. But it is also descriptive of individual local churches. As part of the larger church, every local congregation is itself the Lord's possession—so far as it consists of true believers. Remembering that fact was a powerful motivation for Paul. It should be for us also. After all, what greater privilege could there be than serving in God's own work?

The church is God's possession because it is made up of redeemed saints, each of whom belongs to Him. It is not a physical building,

but a congregation of sinners saved by grace and bought by Christ.
Believers love the church because they were purchased into it, being
made part of it by the Master who owns them. Having given themselves to the Lord, they are eager to give themselves to His people.
To quote again from Spurgeon:

> If you have given yourself to the Lord, give yourself,
> next, to His people, that you may, with them, bear wit-
> ness for Christ. Here is a certain number of people who,
> with all their faults, are the true followers of Christ. Join
> them and say, "I, too, am a follower of Christ." That is
> what membership with the Church means. It is as if you
> should say, "If the world is divided into two camps, I am
> on the side of King Jesus, and under His banner I will
> fight as one of those who bear witness to the Truths of
> God that He has revealed."[2]

The church is the Lord's unique possession. What a privilege it
is for us to be a part!

IMITATING PAUL'S LOVE FOR THE CHURCH

We are greatly blessed to stand on the shoulders of those who
have walked before us in the faith and set an example for us to follow. In regard to our love for the church, the apostle Paul is a model
we ought to emulate (cf. 1 Corinthians 11:1). He loved the church
because he was controlled by the love of Christ, concerned about
the needs of the saints, and captivated by the unique privilege he
had to be involved in advancing God's kingdom. Paul's perspective
should be ours as well. God designed the church so that every member would contribute to the whole (1 Corinthians 12:14-26). That
includes us! The Lord not only saved us from sin and made us one
of His own, but He offers us the opportunity to serve one another
in His household. In light of that privilege, how could any Christian not love the church?

APPENDIXES

Appendix 1

Real Men Pursue Purity

BILL SHANNON

The moral climate of American culture is getting worse and worse. The age of entertainment has ushered in a whole new set of temptations—via movies, television, and the Internet. For Christian men, the call to purity has never been more timely or more necessary. In this short lesson, we will consider five warnings for those who might find themselves tempted by pornography and other forms of sexual sin. Then, at the end, we will briefly discuss five action steps for experiencing victory in this area of life.

FIVE WARNINGS

Warning 1: Beware Lest You Fall

In 1 Peter 5:8, the apostle Peter instructed his readers with these words: "Be of sober spirit, be on the alert. Your adversary, the devil, prowls around like a roaring lion, seeking someone to devour." That verse is a vital call to alertness, especially in the area of moral purity. Note that Peter used two imperatives in his warning: "be sober" and "be alert." Those two commands call us to immediate action. The lives of godly men are characterized by self-control and a spiritual watchfulness that is always on guard against the enemy.

Men of purity take their adversary seriously. Satan is cunning, and he knows that our flesh is weak. The devil has been in the temptation business for a long time. He is relentlessly on the prowl, and subtlety is his modus operandi. Usually the temptation does not come from somewhere obvious, but somewhere unexpected—such as an advertising insert in the newspaper or a magazine at the grocery store checkout stand. That's why the godly man must always be ready to resist temptation and guard his heart and mind.

Not only does Satan prowl about but he is also "seeking someone to devour." His goal is the total destruction of his victims. The phrase "like a roaring lion" portrays how determined the devil is in his activity against believers. The systems of the world have been flooded with smut to lure men away from a life of devotion to Jesus Christ.

Christian men need to take the warnings of Scripture seriously. Satan is proactive in his temptations. Believers must be equally proactive in putting on the armor of God and standing firm against the devil's fiery darts (Ephesians 6:10-17).

Warning 2: Lust Is a Serious Sin

In Matthew 5:27-28, Jesus told His hearers, "You have heard that it was said, 'You shall not commit adultery; but I say to you that everyone who looks at a woman with lust for her has already committed adultery with her in his heart.'" Our Lord's words make it clear that God treats sins of the heart and mind with great seriousness! We should too.

Lust is never a "secret sin" like so many people believe. God knows (Proverbs 5:20-23; 15:3). And the guilty person knows too, feeling shame and regret for his sinful thoughts or actions. The believer who thinks he can continue to hide his sin will discover that God will not be mocked (Proverbs 28:13). If he does not repent, he can expect the chastisement of the Lord.

The only right response to sinful thoughts is to renew your mind daily in the Word and stay as far away from potential temptation as you can. Make no provision for the flesh (Romans 13:14). This may mean no television or movies or Internet, even for an extended period of time. It may necessitate changing certain routines or no longer spending time with certain people. It will also include a willingness to be held accountable, a point we will discuss later.

Lust is a form of idolatry. It is inherently self-centered and the polar opposite of love. It does not seek to serve others, but only to serve itself. If left unchecked, it will inevitably lead to ruin. As James explained in his epistle, "Each one is tempted when he is carried away and enticed by his own lust. Then when lust has conceived, it gives birth to sin; and when sin is accomplished, it brings forth death" (James 1:14-15).

The battle against lust begins in the mind. It is there that the war for purity must be won.

Warning 3: The Lord Is the Avenger

Read what the apostle Paul told the Thessalonians:

> This is the will of God, your sanctification: that you abstain from sexual immorality; that each one of you know how to control his own body in holiness and honor, not in the passion of lust like the Gentiles who do not know God; that no one transgress and wrong his brother in this matter, because the Lord is an avenger in all these things, as we told you beforehand and solemnly warned you. For God has not called us for impurity, but in holiness (1 Thessalonians 4:3-7 ESV).

The pagan cities of the first-century Roman world were characterized by rampant immorality. And Paul instructed believers to stay completely away from that kind of impurity. Instead, they were to exercise self-control and exhibit holiness.

As one commentator has explained about the above passage:

> Christians must not lower themselves to a level of pagan sexual behavior determined merely by unthinking

passions and uncontrolled fleshly urges. Because of
their intimate relationship with a holy God, believers
must not subject themselves to an ungodly society's vast
array of sexually immoral temptations (cf. 2 Timothy
2:22; 1 John 2:15-16). Overexposure to such temptations
will only lower one's resistance and diminish one's out-
rage, thus weakening spiritual resolve and virtue. Scripture warns God's children to stay far away from—and
to flee—all immorality (1 Corinthians 6:18). Lustful
thoughts and feelings can lead believers to actions that
are completely incongruous with their position in the
body of Christ (see 1 Corinthians 6:15-20).[1]

Notice in 1 Thessalonians 4:6 that God is the avenger of those
who persist in sexual sin. He will chastise those who do not repent,
often allowing them to experience devastating consequences as a
result of their foolish choices. The prospect of the Lord's swift punishment should serve as a sobering deterrent to any who might be
tempted in this way.

In verse 7, a positive reason is given as to why believers should
not allow themselves to be stained by immorality. They have been
called by God for the purpose of purity and sanctification. The Lord
has called His people to holiness! Conversely, He commands them
to reject all forms of moral uncleanness.

Paul concluded this paragraph with a final warning: "So, he who
rejects this is not rejecting man but the God who gives His Holy
Spirit to you." Those who ignore the call to moral purity simultaneously rebuff the Lord's authority. Any so-called Christian who per-
sists in sinful behavior would do well to consider whether or not he
is truly in the faith (cf. 2 Corinthians 13:5; Galatians 5:19-21).

Warning 4: Sexual Sin Destroys Its Victims

Consider the following verses from the book of Proverbs:

Proverbs 5:3-5—The lips of an adulteress drip honey and

smoother than oil is her speech; but in the end she is bitter as wormwood, sharp as a two-edged sword. Her feet go down to death, her steps take hold of Sheol.

Proverbs 5:20-23—Why should you, my son, be exhilarated with an adulteress and embrace the bosom of a foreigner? For the ways of a man are before the eyes of the LORD, and He watches all his paths. His own iniquities will capture the wicked, and he will be held with the cords of his sin. He will die for lack of instruction, and in the greatness of his folly he will go astray.

Proverbs 6:32-33—The one who commits adultery with a woman is lacking sense; he who would destroy himself does it. Wounds and disgrace he will find, and his reproach will not be blotted out.

Proverbs 7:22-27—[A foolish man] follows [a harlot] as an ox goes to the slaughter, or as fetters to the discipline of a fool, until an arrow pierces through his liver; as a bird hastens to the snare, so he does not know that it will cost him his life. Now therefore, my sons, listen to me, and pay attention to the words of my mouth. Do not let your heart turn aside to her ways, do not stray into her paths. For many are the victims she has cast down, and numerous are all her slain. Her house is the way to Sheol, descending to the chambers of death.

As these passages make abundantly clear, the path of impurity is a road that leads to destruction. Those who follow it do so to their own demise.

Warning 5: Moral Perversion Degrades and Enslaves

In Romans 1:18-32, Paul described the downward spiral that occurs when a society rejects the true God. Part of that descent includes moral perversion. In relation to the unrighteous, Paul wrote, "Even though they knew God, they did not honor Him as

God or give thanks, but they became futile in their speculations, and their foolish heart was darkened…Therefore God gave them over in the lusts of their hearts to impurity, so that their bodies would be dishonored among them" (verses 21,24).

Those verses describe unbelievers. So when Christians imbibe the filth of the unsaved culture, they are acting just like pagans! The immorality that characterizes secular society is a result of their collective rejection of God. They do not honor Him or give thanks. The professing Christian who is caught in the web of impurity manifests that same spirit of ungratefulness.

Failure to glorify God and give Him thanks will lead one's mind to become darkened and irrational. In the words of one author, "The foolish heart that rejects and dishonors God does not become enlightened and freed…but rather becomes spiritually darkened and further enslaved to sin…Spiritual darkness and moral perversity are inseparable. When man forfeits God, he forfeits virtue."[2] The more a man gives in to this kind of temptation, the more enslaved and degraded he becomes. That is why it is so important for Christian men to flee immorality (1 Corinthians 6:18).

FIVE ACTION STEPS

Those who have sinned in this area need to recognize the seriousness of what they have done and repent. The following five action steps (developed only briefly here) will help them turn from their sin and find victory in this area of their lives.

Step 1: *Admit Your Sin and Take Full Responsibility*

Real change cannot happen until you are willing to repent of your sin and submit to God's Word. Repentance includes confession—admitting that you were wrong and that you need both God's forgiveness (Psalm 51:4) and His help (cf. 1 Corinthians 10:13). Acknowledge the root of your sin, which is self-love. Such idolatry must be recognized for what it is and forsaken. Then rejoice in the reality of God's forgiveness (1 John 1:9), and commit yourself to walking in purity.

Step 2: Acknowledge that Lust Is a Lie

Temptation is built on false promises. The idea that fulfillment can be found in a fantasy (or anywhere outside of God's parameters) is absolutely untrue. Only God can truly satisfy. Lasting joy and true happiness come only from Him—as we live in keeping with His commands. When you accept this truth, you will have made a precious discovery. It will help you guard your heart the next time temptation comes knocking. Like a stereotypical used-car salesman, temptation makes big promises. But in the end, what he's selling is nothing more than junk.

Step 3: Alter Your Lifestyle to Avoid Temptation

Sometimes repentance requires a radical life change. That is often true when the sin is particularly enslaving. So change your routines and do whatever it takes to avoid potential temptation. Start renewing your mind by memorizing and meditating on Scripture. Listen to sermons and worship music. Crowd out sinful thoughts by filling your mind with that which is right, holy, and good (Philippians 4:8). The goal is to put off the sin by making no provision for its entry into your life.

Step 4: Anchor Your Heart in the Word of God

The process of change must take root in your devotional life. Otherwise it will not last. Sins of the heart require more than superficial changes to external behaviors. They require heart renewal, and that happens only as the Spirit of God uses His Word to change your heart (Hebrews 4:12). Your mind must be held captive by the things of Christ and His Word. Let biblical truth dwell in you richly (Colossians 3:16), and recognize that God's Word is the sword of the Spirit, given to help you fend off temptation (Ephesians 6:17).

Through Bible reading and prayer, discipline yourself for holy living (1 Timothy 4:7). As Galatians 5:16 says, "Walk by the Spirit, and you will not carry out the desire of the flesh." Pursue righteousness and integrity as the course of your life. Look to Christ (Hebrews 12:1-2). And maintain a healthy fear of the Lord (Proverbs 14:27).

Step 5: Ask Others to Hold You Accountable

Finally, find a godly man you can trust and have him keep you accountable. If you are married, ask your wife for help too. Make sure to find accountability partners who are not afraid to ask you tough questions and who know you well enough to tell when you are lying. If the goal is victory over sin, you must be willing to do whatever it takes to make that happen. Asking others to help you is nothing to be embarrassed about. Rather, it is a vital aspect of the Christian life (Galatians 6:1).

Remember that you bear the name of Christ. For the sake of your testimony and your usefulness to His kingdom, do whatever it takes to put away the sin that is pulling you downward and start walking in godliness.

Questions for Personal Study or Group Discussion

CHAPTER I—
REAL MEN LIVE BY FAITH (ABRAHAM)

1. What is the most interesting fact you learned about Abraham in this chapter?

2. In your estimation, what event in Abraham's life was the greatest evidence of his faith?

3. Based upon the example of Abraham, what is the key to exercising faith in the face of an uncertain future?

4. Is your faith predominantly characterized by trusting God's plan, justice, timing, and provision? Why, or why not?

5. Are there areas of your life that would keep you from being described as a man who walks by faith? What will you do about them?

6. What is the relationship between faith and salvation?

7. Read through the Scripture passages for this chapter in the Biblical Reference Guide. As you do, discuss how each passage affirms, clarifies, or applies the truths you learned from reading this chapter. Are there other verses that also come to mind?

CHAPTER 2—
REAL MEN FIND SATISFACTION
IN GOD (SOLOMON)

1. What is the most interesting fact you learned about Solomon from reading this chapter?

2. What are some of the past pursuits in your life that you hoped would bring you happiness?

3. According to this chapter, where does the pursuit of satisfaction by worldly means end?

4. Does God desire for His people to be satisfied? Why?

5. What is the means of satisfaction that God has provided?

6. Where does the compass of your heart point? What adjustments, if any, need to be made?

7. Read through the Scripture passages for this chapter in the Biblical Reference Guide. As you do, discuss how each passage affirms, clarifies, or applies the truths you learned from reading this chapter. Are there other verses that also come to mind?

Chapter 3—
REAL MEN TREASURE GOD'S WORD
(JOSIAH)

1. What is the most interesting fact you learned about Josiah from reading this chapter?

2. What is it about the Bible that makes it a treasure worth preserving?

3. What actions can you take to affirm that you truly believe the Scriptures are a treasure?

4. How would those who know you best describe your attitude toward the Scriptures?

5. How can you be sure to apply God's Word to your own life on a more regular basis?

6. As a man (and perhaps a husband and father), what steps are you taking to ensure that the truth of God's Word is not lost to your family?

7. Read through the Scripture passages for this chapter in the Biblical Reference Guide. As you do, discuss how each passage affirms, clarifies, or applies the truths you learned from reading this chapter. Are there other verses that also come to mind?

CHAPTER 4—
REAL MEN PRAY WITH BOLDNESS
(ELIJAH)

1. What is the most interesting fact you learned about Elijah from reading this chapter?

2. According to this chapter, what motivated the prayer life of Elijah?

3. What is the greatest hindrance to your prayer life? What will you do to overcome that difficulty?

4. Are your prayers characterized by earnestness, frequency, humility, and boldness? Why or why not?

5. Why is it significant that James described Elijah as a man just like us? How is that fact encouraging?

6. Read through the Scripture passages for this chapter in the Biblical Reference Guide. As you do, discuss how each passage affirms, clarifies, or applies the truths you learned from reading this chapter. Are there other verses that also come to mind?

CHAPTER 5—
REAL MEN LOVE TO WORSHIP
(HYMN WRITERS OF ISRAEL)

1. The book of Psalms was written by many different authors. It is one of the most beloved books in the Bible. What is your favorite psalm? Why?

2. What are the characteristics of true worship?

3. What is the difference between worship and music? Why do you think the two are so often confused?

4. How would you rate your worship? What can you do to begin worshiping God the way He intends for you to worship Him?

5. Why should the cross be central to a life of worship? What does Revelation 4–5 indicate about our future as worshipers?

6. Read through the Scripture passages for this chapter in the Biblical Reference Guide. As you do, discuss how each passage affirms, clarifies, or applies the truths you learned from reading this chapter. Are there other verses that also come to mind?

Chapter 6—
REAL MEN FLEE TEMPTATION
(TIMOTHY)

1. What is the most interesting fact you learned about Timothy from reading this chapter?

2. According to the definitions put forward in this chapter, how are you doing in pursuing a lifestyle of masculine self-denial? Where do you see room for improvement?

3. What is the right response to temptation?

4. What steps have you taken in your own life to flee temptation? What steps should you be ready to take during future times of temptation?

5. What are some of the most common temptations that Christian men face? After reading this chapter, what advice would you give a friend who was struggling with those temptations?

6. Read through the Scripture passages for this chapter in the Biblical Reference Guide. As you do, discuss how each passage affirms, clarifies, or applies the truths you learned from reading this chapter. Are there other verses that also come to mind?

CHAPTER 7—
REAL MEN REPENT FROM SIN
(DAVID)

1. What is the most interesting fact you learned about David from reading this chapter?

2. Why did David wait so long to repent?

3. According to this chapter, what is the defining mark of genuine repentance?

4. Why is repentance so important? Practically speaking, what would repentance look like in the life of a Christian man?

5. Even after repentance, a person may still experience painful consequences that result from the sin committed. What is the appropriate response to those consequences?

6. Read through the Scripture passages for this chapter in the Biblical Reference Guide. As you do, discuss how each passage affirms, clarifies, or applies the truths you learned from reading this chapter. Are there other verses that also come to mind?

CHAPTER 8—
REAL MEN REFUSE TO COMPROMISE
(DANIEL)

1. What is the most interesting fact you learned about Daniel from reading this chapter?

2. List some ways in which Daniel could have compromised. How would those compromises have changed his legacy?

3. What enabled Daniel to maintain his integrity in the face of a hostile environment? How do you think you would have responded if you had been in his place?

4. What are the first steps toward compromise? What can you do to guard against taking such steps?

5. According to this chapter, what is necessary in order to live a life free of compromise?

6. If integrity is defined as a lifetime of right choices (consistent conviction), what would integrity look like in your own life?

7. Read through the Scripture passages for this chapter in the Biblical Reference Guide. As you do, discuss how each passage affirms, clarifies, or applies the truths you learned from reading this chapter. Are there other verses that also come to mind?

CHAPTER 9—
REAL MEN LEAD WITH COURAGE
(NEHEMIAH)

1. What is the most interesting fact you learned about Nehemiah from reading this chapter?

2. In what ways did Nehemiah evidence courage and leadership?

3. According to the story of Nehemiah, how does a reliance upon God translate into strength of leadership? In your own life, how does your faith affect your courage?

4. Why is steadfast conviction critical to leading with courage? What are some convictions you would like to strengthen in your life?

5. When the exercise of courageous leadership requires sacrifice, are you a man who is willing to proceed? Is there a point at which a Christian man should consider that sacrifice to be "too high"? Why or why not?

6. Read through the Scripture passages for this chapter in the Biblical Reference Guide. As you do, discuss how each passage affirms, clarifies, or applies the truths you learned from reading this chapter. Are there other verses that also come to mind?

CHAPTER 10—
REAL MEN LOVE THEIR WIVES
(PETER)

1. What is the most interesting fact you learned about Peter from reading this chapter?

2. According to this chapter, what was the key catalyst in Peter's life that allowed him to properly love his wife? Why is that significant?

3. If you are married, in what ways does your knowledge and reflection of God draw your wife toward the Lord? What practical things are you doing—or can you do— to shepherd her heart in Christlikeness?

4. If you asked your wife whether she felt you showed her the proper understanding and honor, what would her response be? In what areas do you think you could do better?

5. In what ways should your love for your wife model the love of Christ?

6. Read through the Scripture passages for this chapter in the Biblical Reference Guide. As you do, discuss how each passage affirms, clarifies, or applies the truths you learned from reading this chapter. Are there other verses that also come to mind?

CHAPTER 11—
REAL MEN SHEPHERD THEIR FAMILIES (EPHESIANS 5–6)

1. If you are a father, how would you describe your home? Are you being faithful to treat it as the mission field that it is?

2. Are there any aspects of your parenting that could be described as proud, inattentive, or angry? If so, what will you do to change those things?

3. In what ways have you viewed the position of shepherd of your home as a burden, and in what ways have you viewed it as a privilege? What heart attitudes can you cultivate so that you view your position more and more as a privilege?

4. Does the thought of giving an account to the Lord for your parenting reenergize your efforts, or cause you great fear? Why?

5. What can you do to increase your efforts to shepherd your family in a way that honors God? How do you plan to initiate these changes?

6. Read through the Scripture passages for this chapter in the Biblical Reference Guide. As you do, discuss how each passage affirms, clarifies, or applies the truths you learned from reading this chapter. Are there other verses that also come to mind?

Chapter 12—
REAL MEN WORK HARD
(PROVERBS)

1. What areas in your life could be described as "slug-gardly"?

2. Why is it important for Christian men to study Proverbs and its warnings to the sluggard? After reading this chapter, what counsel would you give to a friend who shows a propensity toward laziness?

3. Do you view work as a blessing or a curse? What is the right way to think about work?

4. List some ways that work is a gift from God.

5. What goal in your life motivates you to work? Is that goal a godly one? What differentiates a Christian motivation to work from a worldly one?

6. Read through the Scripture passages for this chapter in the Biblical Reference Guide. As you do, discuss how each passage affirms, clarifies, or applies the truths you learned from reading this chapter. Are there other verses that also come to mind?

CHAPTER 13—
REAL MEN LOVE THEIR ENEMIES
(ELISHA)

1. What is the most interesting fact you learned about Elisha from reading this chapter?

2. According to Scripture, is there ever an appropriate reason not to love your enemies? Why is it difficult to demonstrate love to an enemy?

3. Whom would you think of as an enemy? Practically speaking, what can you do to show love to that individual or those people?

4. In what ways should your attitude toward your enemies reflect the attitude of Christ? How did He respond to those who hated Him?

5. The most important way you can show love to your enemy is to share the good news of the gospel with him. Why is that?

6. Read through the Scripture passages for this chapter in the Biblical Reference Guide. As you do, discuss how each passage affirms, clarifies, or applies the truths you learned from reading this chapter. Are there other verses that also come to mind?

Chapter 14—
REAL MEN SHARE THE GOSPEL
(ACTS)

1. Why do many Christians find it difficult to share the gospel? What is the biggest challenge for you personally?

2. What does an unwillingness to share the gospel reveal about a person's relationship to Christ? What must change within your life in order for your passion for evangelism to increase?

3. In your gospel presentation, what role should the message of repentance play? How would you explain the gospel to an unbeliever?

4. As a man and godly leader of your home, what can you do to communicate to the rest of your family that evangelism is important? If you are not doing those things, what steps can you take to change that?

5. As we saw in the chapter, the proclamation of the gospel requires personal sacrifice. What should your response be to that reality?

6. Read through the Scripture passages for this chapter in the Biblical Reference Guide. As you do, discuss how each passage affirms, clarifies, or applies the truths you learned from reading this chapter. Are there other verses that also come to mind?

CHAPTER 15—
REAL MEN LOVE THE CHURCH
(PAUL)

1. What is the most interesting fact you learned about Paul from reading this chapter?

2. What does a person's attitude toward the church reveal about the condition of his heart?

3. In one sentence, how would you describe Paul's attitude toward the church?

4. According to this chapter, what motivated Paul's love for the church? To what extent do you see those same motivations in your own life? Where is there room for improvement?

5. Do problems within the local church justify a distaste for the local church? How would a godly man respond to the presence of problems in his church?

6. What are you doing—or could you be doing—to help serve as a positive influence in your church?

7. Read through the Scripture passages for this chapter in the Biblical Reference Guide. As you do, discuss how each passage affirms, clarifies, or applies the truths you learned from reading this chapter. Are there other verses that also come to mind?

BIBLICAL
REFERENCE
GUIDE

Biblical Reference Guide

This guide contains Scripture verses related to the themes addressed in this book. Though the list is not exhaustive, our hope is that it will encourage you toward greater growth as a man of the Word.

FOREWORD:
REAL MEN WALK WITH GOD

Genesis 5:24—Enoch walked with God; and he was not, for God took him.

Genesis 6:9—These are the records of the generations of Noah. Noah was a righteous man, blameless in his time; Noah walked with God.

Genesis 17:1—Now when Abram was ninety-nine years old, the Lord appeared to Abram and said to him, "I am God Almighty; walk before Me, and be blameless."

Deuteronomy 8:6—You shall keep the commandments of the Lord your God, to walk in His ways and to fear Him.

Joshua 22:5—Be very careful to observe the commandment and the law which Moses the servant of the LORD commanded you, to love the LORD your God and walk in all His ways and keep His commandments and hold fast to Him and serve Him with all your heart and with all your soul.

1 Kings 2:1-3—As David's time to die drew near, he charged Solomon his son, saying, "I am going the way of all the earth. Be strong, therefore, and show yourself a man. Keep the charge of the LORD your God, to walk in His ways, to keep His statutes, His commandments, His ordinances, and His testimonies, according to what is written in the Law of Moses, that you may succeed in all that you do and wherever you turn."

2 Kings 23:3—The king [Josiah] stood by the pillar and made a covenant before the LORD, to walk after the LORD, and to keep His commandments and His testimonies and His statutes with all his heart and all his soul, to carry out the words of this covenant that were written in this book. And all the people entered into the covenant.

Psalm 119:2-3—How blessed are those who observe His testimonies, who seek Him with all their heart. They also do no unrighteousness; they walk in His ways.

Galatians 6:16,22-25—Walk by the Spirit, and you will not carry out the desire of the flesh…the fruit of the Spirit is love, joy, peace, patience, kindness, goodness, faithfulness, gentleness, self-control; against such things there is no law. Now those who belong to Christ Jesus have crucified the flesh with its passions and desires. If we live by the Spirit, let us also walk by the Spirit.

Ephesians 4:1—I, the prisoner of the Lord, implore you to walk in a manner worthy of the calling with which you have been called.

Colossians 1:9-10—We have not ceased to pray for you and to ask that you may be filled with the knowledge of His will in all spiritual wisdom and understanding, so that you will walk in a manner worthy of the Lord, to please Him in all respects, bearing fruit in every good work and increasing in the knowledge of God.

Hebrews 11:5—By faith Enoch was taken up so that he would not see death; and he was not found because God took him up; for he obtained the witness that before his being taken up he was pleasing to God.

I.

REAL MEN LIVE BY FAITH
(ABRAHAM)

Genesis 15:6—Then [Abraham] believed in the Lord; and He reckoned it to him as righteousness.

Psalm 32:10-11—Many are the sorrows of the wicked, but he who trusts in the Lord, lovingkindness shall surround him. Be glad in the Lord and rejoice, you righteous ones; and shout for joy, all you who are upright in heart.

Psalm 56:3-4—When I am afraid, I will put my trust in You. In God, whose word I praise, in God I have put my trust; I shall not be afraid. What can mere man do to me?

Proverbs 3:5-6—Trust in the Lord with all your heart and do not lean on your own understanding. In all your ways acknowledge Him, and He will make your paths straight.

Proverbs 28:25-26—An arrogant man stirs up strife, but he who trusts in the Lord will prosper. He who trusts in his own heart is a fool, but he who walks wisely will be delivered.

Habakkuk 2:4—Behold, as for the proud one, his soul is not right within him; but the righteous will live by his faith.

Romans 5:1-2—Therefore, having been justified by faith, we have peace with God through our Lord Jesus Christ, through whom also we have obtained our introduction by faith into this grace in which we stand; and we exult in hope of the glory of God.

Ephesians 2:8-10—For by grace you have been saved through faith; and that not of yourselves, it is the gift of God; not as a result of works, so that no one may boast. For we are His workmanship, created in Christ Jesus for good works, which God prepared beforehand so that we would walk in them.

Hebrews 11:1-2,6—Now faith is the assurance of things hoped for, the conviction of things not seen. For by it the men of old gained approval...And without faith it is impossible to please Him, for he who comes to God must believe that He is and that He is a rewarder of those who seek Him.

Hebrews 11:8-19—By faith Abraham, when he was called, obeyed by going out to a place which he was to receive for an inheritance; and he went out, not knowing where he was going. By faith he lived as an alien in the land of promise, as in a foreign land, dwelling in tents with Isaac and Jacob, fellow heirs of the same promise; for he was looking for the city which has foundations, whose architect and builder is God. By faith even Sarah herself received ability to conceive, even beyond the proper time of life, since she considered Him faithful who had promised. Therefore there was born even of one man, and him as good as dead at that, as many descendants as the stars of heaven in number, and innumerable as the sand which is by the seashore.

All these died in faith, without receiving the promises, but having seen them and having welcomed them from a distance, and having confessed that they were strangers and exiles on the earth. For those who say such things make it clear that they are seeking a country of their own. And indeed if they had been thinking of that country from which they went out, they would have had opportunity to return. But as it is, they desire a better country, that is, a heavenly one. Therefore God is not ashamed to be called their God; for He has prepared a city for them.

By faith Abraham, when he was tested, offered up Isaac, and he who had received the promises was offering up his only begotten son; it was he to whom it was said, "In Isaac your descendants shall be called." He considered that God is able to raise people even from the dead, from which he also received him back as a type.

2.
REAL MEN FIND SATISFACTION
IN GOD (SOLOMON)

Psalm 34:8-10—O taste and see that the LORD is good; how blessed is the man who takes refuge in Him! O fear the LORD, you His saints; for to those who fear Him there is no want. The young lions do lack and suffer hunger; but they who seek the LORD shall not be in want of any good thing.

Psalm 37:4-6,16,28—Delight yourself in the LORD; and He will give you the desires of your heart. Commit your way to the LORD, trust also in Him, and He will do it. He will bring forth your righteousness as the light and your judgment as the noonday...Better is the little of the righteous than the abundance of many wicked...For the LORD loves justice and does not forsake His godly ones; they are preserved forever, but the descendants of the wicked will be cut off.

Psalm 103:2-5—Bless the LORD, O my soul, and forget none of His benefits; who pardons all your iniquities, who heals all your diseases; who redeems your life from the pit, who crowns you with lovingkindness and compassion; who satisfies your years with good things, so that your youth is renewed like the eagle.

Ecclesiastes 5:10—He who loves money will not be satisfied with money, nor he who loves abundance with its income. This too is vanity.

Ecclesiastes 11:9—Rejoice, young man, during your childhood, and let your heart be pleasant during the days of young manhood. And follow the impulses of your heart and the desires of your eyes. Yet know that God will bring you to judgment for all these things.

Matthew 11:28-30—Come to Me, all who are weary and heavy-laden, and I will give you rest. Take My yoke upon you and learn from Me, for I am gentle and humble in heart, and you will find rest for your souls. For My yoke is easy and My burden is light.

John 6:35,40—Jesus said to them, "I am the bread of life; he who comes to Me will not hunger, and he who believes in Me will never thirst…For this is the will of My Father, that everyone who beholds the Son and believes in Him will have eternal life, and I Myself will raise him up on the last day."

Philippians 3:7-11—Whatever things were gain to me, those things I have counted as loss for the sake of Christ. More than that, I count all things to be loss in view of the surpassing value of knowing Christ Jesus my Lord, for whom I have suffered the loss of all things, and count them but rubbish so that I may gain Christ, and may be found in Him, not having a righteousness of my own derived from the Law, but that which is through faith in Christ, the righteousness which comes from God on the basis of faith, that I may know Him and the power of His resurrection and the fellowship of His sufferings, being conformed to His death; in order that I may attain to the resurrection from the dead.

3.

REAL MEN TREASURE
GOD'S WORD (JOSIAH)

Psalm 1:1-3—How blessed is the man who does not walk in the counsel of the wicked, nor stand in the path of sinners, nor sit in the seat of scoffers! But his delight is in the law of the LORD, and in His law he meditates day and night. He will be like a tree firmly planted by streams of water, which yields its fruit in its season and its leaf does not wither; and in whatever he does, he prospers.

Psalm 19:7-11—The law of the LORD is perfect, restoring the soul; the testimony of the LORD is sure, making wise the simple. The precepts of the LORD are right, rejoicing the heart; the commandment of the LORD is pure, enlightening the eyes. The fear of the LORD is clean, enduring forever; the judgments of the LORD are true; they are righteous altogether. They are more desirable than gold, yes, than much fine gold; sweeter also than honey and the drippings of the honeycomb. Moreover, by them Your servant is warned; in keeping them there is great reward.

Psalm 119:103-105—How sweet are Your words to my taste! Yes, sweeter than honey to my mouth! From Your precepts I get understanding; therefore I hate every false way. Your word is a lamp to my feet and a light to my path.

Isaiah 66:1-2—Thus says the LORD, "Heaven is My throne and the earth is My footstool. Where then is a house you could build for Me? And where is a place that I may rest? For My hand made all these things, thus all these things came into being," declares the LORD. "But to this one I will look, to him who is humble and contrite of spirit, and who trembles at My word."

John 17:17—Sanctify them in the truth; Your word is truth.

Ephesians 6:13,17—Take up the full armor of God, so that you will be able to resist in the evil day, and having done everything, to stand firm…And take the helmet of salvation, and the sword of the Spirit, which is the word of God.

Hebrews 4:12—The word of God is living and active and sharper than any two-edged sword, and piercing as far as the division of soul and spirit, of both joints and marrow, and able to judge the thoughts and intentions of the heart.

James 1:21-25—Putting aside all filthiness and all that remains of wickedness, in humility receive the word implanted, which is able to save your souls. But prove yourselves doers of the word, and not merely hearers who delude themselves. For if anyone is a hearer of the word and not a doer, he is like a man who looks at his natural face in a mirror; for once he has looked at himself and gone away, he has immediately forgotten what kind of person he was. But one who looks intently at the perfect law, the law of liberty, and abides by it, not having become a forgetful hearer but an effectual doer, this man will be blessed in what he does.

1 Peter 2:1-3—Putting aside all malice and all deceit and hypocrisy and envy and all slander, like newborn babies, long for the pure milk of the word, so that by it you may grow in respect to salvation, if you have tasted the kindness of the Lord.

4.
REAL MEN PRAY WITH BOLDNESS
(ELIJAH)

Proverbs 15:8,29—The sacrifice of the wicked is an abomination to the Lord, but the prayer of the upright is His delight...The Lord is far from the wicked, but He hears the prayer of the righteous.

Matthew 7:7-11—Ask, and it will be given to you; seek, and you will find; knock, and it will be opened to you. For everyone who asks receives, and he who seeks finds, and to him who knocks it will be opened. Or what man is there among you who, when his son asks for a loaf, will give him a stone? Or if he asks for a fish, he will not give him a snake, will he? If you then, being evil, know how to give good gifts to your children, how much more will your Father who is in heaven give what is good to those who ask Him!

Ephesians 6:18—With all prayer and petition pray at all times in the Spirit, and with this in view, be on the alert with all perseverance and petition for all the saints.

Philippians 4:6-7—Be anxious for nothing, but in everything by prayer and supplication with thanksgiving let your requests be made known to God. And the peace of God, which surpasses all comprehension, will guard your hearts and your minds in Christ Jesus.

1 Thessalonians 5:16-18—Rejoice always; pray without ceasing; in everything give thanks; for this is God's will for you in Christ Jesus.

1 Timothy 2:1,8—First of all, then, I urge that entreaties and prayers, petitions and thanksgivings, be made on behalf of all men…Therefore I want the men in every place to pray, lifting up holy hands, without wrath and dissension.

James 1:5-6—If any of you lacks wisdom, let him ask of God, who gives to all generously and without reproach, and it will be given to him. But he must ask in faith without any doubting, for the one who doubts is like the surf of the sea, driven and tossed by the wind.

James 5:16-18—The effective prayer of a righteous man can accomplish much. Elijah was a man with a nature like ours, and he prayed earnestly that it would not rain, and it did not rain on the earth for three years and six months. Then he prayed again, and the sky poured rain and the earth produced its fruit.

1 John 5:14-15—This is the confidence which we have before Him, that, if we ask anything according to His will, He hears us. And if we know that He hears us in whatever we ask, we know that we have the requests which we have asked from Him.

5.

REAL MEN LOVE TO WORSHIP
(HYMN WRITERS OF ISRAEL)

Exodus 20:3-6—You shall have no other gods before Me. You shall not make for yourself an idol, or any likeness of what is in heaven above or on the earth beneath or in the water under the earth. You shall not worship them or serve them; for I, the LORD your God, am a jealous God, visiting the iniquity of the fathers on the children, on the third and the fourth generations of those who hate Me, but showing lovingkindness to thousands, to those who love Me and keep My commandments.

Psalm 2:11-12—Worship the LORD with reverence and rejoice with trembling. Do homage to the Son, that He not become angry, and you perish in the way, for His wrath may soon be kindled. How blessed are all who take refuge in Him!

Psalm 29:1-4—Ascribe to the LORD, O sons of the mighty, ascribe to the LORD glory and strength. Ascribe to the LORD the glory due to His name; worship the LORD in holy array. The voice of the LORD is upon the waters; the God of glory thunders, the LORD is over many waters. The voice of the LORD is powerful, the voice of the LORD is majestic.

Psalm 95:6-7—Come, let us worship and bow down, let us kneel before the LORD our Maker. For He is our God, and we are the people of His pasture and the sheep of His hand.

Romans 12:1-2—I urge you, brethren, by the mercies of God, to present your bodies a living and holy sacrifice, acceptable to God, which is your spiritual service of worship. And do not be conformed to this world, but be transformed by the renewing of your mind, so that you may prove what the will of God is, that which is good and acceptable and perfect.

Ephesians 5:18-20—Do not get drunk with wine, for that is dissipation, but be filled with the Spirit, speaking to one another in psalms and hymns and spiritual songs, singing and making melody with your heart to the Lord; always giving thanks for all things in the name of our Lord Jesus Christ to God, even the Father.

Hebrews 13:15-16—Through Him then, let us continually offer up a sacrifice of praise to God, that is, the fruit of lips that give thanks to His name. And do not neglect doing good and sharing, for with such sacrifices God is pleased.

Revelation 4:8-11—The four living creatures, each one of them having six wings, are full of eyes around and within; and day and night they do not cease to say, "Holy, holy, holy is the Lord God, the Almighty, who was and who is and who is to come." And when the living creatures give glory and honor and thanks to Him who sits on the throne, to Him who lives forever and ever, the twenty-four elders will fall down before Him who sits on the throne, and will worship Him who lives forever and ever, and will cast their crowns before the throne, saying, "Worthy are You, our Lord and our God, to receive glory and honor and power; for You created all things, and because of Your will they existed, and were created."

Revelation 5:11-14—I looked, and I heard the voice of many angels around the throne and the living creatures and the elders; and the number of them was myriads of myriads, and thousands of thousands, saying with a loud voice, "Worthy is the Lamb that was slain to receive power and riches and wisdom and might and honor and glory and blessing." And every created thing which is in heaven and on the earth and under the earth and on the sea, and all things in them, I heard saying, "To Him who sits on the throne, and to the Lamb, be blessing and honor and glory and dominion forever and ever." And the four living creatures kept saying, "Amen." And the elders fell down and worshiped.

6.
REAL MEN FLEE TEMPTATION
(TIMOTHY)

Proverbs 1:10,15—My son, if sinners entice you, do not consent…My son, do not walk in the way with them. Keep your feet from their path,

Matthew 6:9-13—Pray, then, in this way: "Our Father who is in heaven, hallowed be Your name. Your kingdom come. Your will be done, on earth as it is in heaven. Give us this day our daily bread. And forgive us our debts, as we also have forgiven our debtors. And do not lead us into temptation, but deliver us from evil. [For Yours is the kingdom and the power and the glory forever. Amen.]"

1 Corinthians 6:18-20—Flee immorality. Every other sin that a man commits is outside the body, but the immoral man sins against his own body. Or do you not know that your body is a temple of the Holy Spirit who is in you, whom you have from God, and that you are not your own? For you have been bought with a price: therefore glorify God in your body.

1 Corinthians 10:13-14—No temptation has overtaken you but such as is common to man; and God is faithful, who will not allow you to be tempted beyond what you are able, but with the temptation will provide the way of escape also, so that you will be able to endure it. Therefore, my beloved, flee from idolatry.

Ephesians 6:10-12—Be strong in the Lord and in the strength of His might. Put on the full armor of God, so that you will be able to stand firm against the schemes of the devil. For our struggle is not against flesh and blood, but against the rulers, against the powers, against the world forces of this darkness, against the spiritual forces of wickedness in the heavenly places.

1 Timothy 6:10-11—The love of money is a root of all sorts of evil, and some by longing for it have wandered away from the faith and pierced themselves with many griefs. But flee from these things, you man of God, and pursue righteousness, godliness, faith, love, perseverance and gentleness.

2 Timothy 2:22—Now flee from youthful lusts and pursue righteousness, faith, love and peace, with those who call on the Lord from a pure heart.

James 4:7-8—Submit therefore to God. Resist the devil and he will flee from you. Draw near to God and He will draw near to you. Cleanse your hands, you sinners; and purify your hearts, you double-minded.

1 Peter 5:8-9—Be of sober spirit, be on the alert. Your adversary, the devil, prowls around like a roaring lion, seeking someone to devour. But resist him, firm in your faith, knowing that the same experiences of suffering are being accomplished by your brethren who are in the world.

1 John 2:15-17—Do not love the world nor the things in the world. If anyone loves the world, the love of the Father is not in him. For all that is in the world, the lust of the flesh and the lust of the eyes and the boastful pride of life, is not from the Father, but is from the world. The world is passing away, and also its lusts; but the one who does the will of God lives forever.

7.
REAL MEN REPENT FROM SIN
(DAVID)

Psalm 32:1-5—How blessed is he whose transgression is forgiven, whose sin is covered! How blessed is the man to whom the LORD does not impute iniquity, and in whose spirit there is no deceit! When I kept silent about my sin, my body wasted away through my groaning all day long. For day and night Your hand was heavy upon me; my vitality was drained away as with the fever heat of summer. I acknowledged my sin to You, and my iniquity I did not hide; I said, "I will confess my transgressions to the LORD"; and You forgave the guilt of my sin.

Psalm 51:1-4—Be gracious to me, O God, according to Your lovingkindness; according to the greatness of Your compassion blot out my transgressions. Wash me thoroughly from my iniquity and cleanse me from my sin. For I know my transgressions, and my sin is ever before me. Against You, You only, I have sinned and done what is evil in Your sight, so that You are justified when You speak and blameless when You judge.

Proverbs 28:13-14—He who conceals his transgressions will not prosper, but he who confesses and forsakes them will find compassion. How blessed is the man who fears always, but he who hardens his heart will fall into calamity.

2 Corinthians 7:9-10—I now rejoice, not that you were made sorrowful, but that you were made sorrowful to the point of repentance; for you were made sorrowful according to the will of God, so that you might not suffer loss in anything through us. For the sorrow that is according to the will of God produces a repentance without regret, leading to salvation, but the sorrow of the world produces death.

Ephesians 4:20-24—You did not learn Christ in this way, if indeed you have heard Him and have been taught in Him, just as truth is in Jesus, that, in reference to your former manner of life, you lay aside the old self, which is being corrupted in accordance with the lusts of deceit, and that you be renewed in the spirit of your mind, and put on the new self, which in the likeness of God has been created in righteousness and holiness of the truth.

2 Timothy 2:24-26—The Lord's bond-servant must not be quarrelsome, but be kind to all, able to teach, patient when wronged, with gentleness correcting those who are in opposition, if perhaps God may grant them repentance leading to the knowledge of the truth, and they may come to their senses and escape from the snare of the devil, having been held captive by him to do his will.

Hebrews 12:1-2—Since we have so great a cloud of witnesses surrounding us, let us also lay aside every encumbrance and the sin which so easily entangles us, and let us run with endurance the race that is set before us, fixing our eyes on Jesus, the author and perfecter of faith, who for the joy set before Him endured the cross, despising the shame, and has sat down at the right hand of the throne of God.

1 John 1:6-9—If we say that we have fellowship with Him and yet walk in the darkness, we lie and do not practice the truth; but if we walk in the Light as He Himself is in the Light, we have fellowship with one another, and the blood of Jesus His Son cleanses us from all sin. If we say that we have no sin, we are deceiving ourselves and the truth is not in us. If we confess our sins, He is faithful and righteous to forgive us our sins and to cleanse us from all unrighteousness.

8.
REAL MEN REFUSE TO COMPROMISE (DANIEL)

Genesis 39:6-10—Now Joseph was handsome in form and appearance. It came about after these events that his master's wife looked with desire at Joseph, and she said, "Lie with me." But he refused and said to his master's wife, "Behold, with me here, my master does not concern himself with anything in the house, and he has put all that he owns in my charge. There is no one greater in this house than I, and he has withheld nothing from me except you, because you are his wife. How then could I do this great evil and sin against God?" As she spoke to Joseph day after day, he did not listen to her to lie beside her or be with her.

Psalm 26:1-5,11—Vindicate me, O LORD, for I have walked in my integrity, and I have trusted in the LORD without wavering. Examine me, O LORD, and try me; test my mind and my heart. For Your lovingkindness is before my eyes, and I have walked in Your truth. I do not sit with deceitful men, nor will I go with pretenders. I hate the assembly of evildoers, and I will not sit with the wicked…But as for me, I shall walk in my integrity; redeem me, and be gracious to me.

Proverbs 4:14-15,18-19—Do not enter the path of the wicked and do not proceed in the way of evil men. Avoid it, do not pass by it; turn away from it and pass on…But the path of the righteous is like the light of dawn, that shines brighter and brighter until the full day. The way of the wicked is like darkness; they do not know over what they stumble.

Proverbs 20:7—A righteous man who walks in his integrity—how blessed are his sons after him.

Proverbs 28:6—Better is the poor who walks in his integrity than he who is crooked though he be rich.

Daniel 1:8—Daniel made up his mind that he would not defile himself with the king's choice food or with the wine which he drank; so he sought permission from the commander of the officials that he might not defile himself.

1 Corinthians 9:24-27—Do you not know that those who run in a race all run, but only one receives the prize? Run in such a way that you may win. Everyone who competes in the games exercises self-control in all things. They then do it to receive a perishable wreath, but we an imperishable. Therefore I run in such a way, as not without aim; I box in such a way, as not beating the air; but I discipline my body and make it my slave, so that, after I have preached to others, I myself will not be disqualified.

2 Timothy 4:7-8—I have fought the good fight, I have finished the course, I have kept the faith; in the future there is laid up for me the crown of righteousness, which the Lord, the righteous Judge, will award to me on that day; and not only to me, but also to all who have loved His appearing.

James 4:4—You adulteresses, do you not know that friendship with the world is hostility toward God? Therefore whoever wishes to be a friend of the world makes himself an enemy of God.

1 Peter 1:14-16—As obedient children, do not be conformed to the former lusts which were yours in your ignorance, but like the Holy One who called you, be holy yourselves also in all your behavior; because it is written, "You shall be holy, for I am holy."

9.
REAL MEN LEAD WITH COURAGE (NEHEMIAH)

Deuteronomy 31:6—Be strong and courageous, do not be afraid or tremble at them, for the LORD your God is the one who goes with you. He will not fail you or forsake you.

Joshua 1:1,6-9—Now it came about after the death of Moses the servant of the LORD, that the LORD spoke to Joshua the son of Nun, Moses' servant, saying… "Be strong and courageous, for you shall give this people possession of the land which I swore to their fathers to give them. Only be strong and very courageous; be careful to do according to all the law which Moses My servant commanded you; do not turn from it to the right or to the left, so that you may have success wherever you go. This book of the law shall not depart from your mouth, but you shall meditate on it day and night, so that you may be careful to do according to all that is written in it; for then you will make your way prosperous, and then you will have success. Have I not commanded you? Be strong and courageous! Do not tremble or be dismayed, for the LORD your God is with you wherever you go."

1 Chronicles 22:11-13—Now, my son, the LORD be with you that you may be successful, and build the house of the LORD your God just as He has spoken concerning you. Only the LORD give you discretion and understanding, and give you charge over Israel, so that you may keep the law of the LORD your God. Then you will prosper, if you are careful to observe the statutes and the ordinances which the LORD commanded Moses concerning Israel. Be strong and courageous, do not fear nor be dismayed.

Psalm 27:13-14—I would have despaired unless I had believed that I would see the goodness of the LORD in the land of the living. Wait for the LORD; be strong and let your heart take courage; yes, wait for the LORD.

Psalm 31:23-24—O love the LORD, all you His godly ones! The LORD preserves the faithful and fully recompenses the proud doer. Be strong and let your heart take courage, all you who hope in the LORD.

1 Corinthians 16:13-14—Be on the alert, stand firm in the faith, act like men, be strong. Let all that you do be done in love.

2 Corinthians 5:6-9—[Be] always of good courage, and [know] that while we are at home in the body we are absent from the Lord—for we walk by faith, not by sight—we are of good courage, I say, and prefer rather to be absent from the body and to be at home with the Lord. Therefore we also have as our ambition, whether at home or absent, to be pleasing to Him.

Philippians 1:20-21—My earnest expectation and hope [is] that I will not be put to shame in anything, but that with all boldness, Christ will even now, as always, be exalted in my body, whether by life or by death. For to me, to live is Christ and to die is gain.

10.
REAL MEN LOVE THEIR WIVES
(PETER)

Genesis 2:22-24—The LORD God fashioned into a woman the rib which He had taken from the man, and brought her to the man. The man said, "This is now bone of my bones, and flesh of my flesh; she shall be called Woman, because she was taken out of Man." For this reason a man shall leave his father and his mother, and be joined to his wife; and they shall become one flesh.

Proverbs 5:15,18-19—Drink water from your own cistern and fresh water from your own well...Let your fountain be blessed, and rejoice in the wife of your youth. As a loving hind and a graceful doe, let her breasts satisfy you at all times; be exhilarated always with her love.

Proverbs 18:22—He who finds a wife finds a good thing and obtains favor from the LORD.

Proverbs 31:10-12,28-30—An excellent wife, who can find? For her worth is far above jewels. The heart of her husband trusts in her, and he will have no lack of gain. She does him good and not evil all the days of her life...Her children rise up and bless her; her husband also, and he praises her, saying: "Many daughters have done nobly, but you excel them all." Charm is deceitful and beauty is vain, but a woman who fears the LORD, she shall be praised.

Ephesians 5:25,28-33—Husbands, love your wives, just as Christ also loved the church...So husbands ought also to love their own wives as their own bodies. He who loves his own wife loves himself; for no one ever hated his own flesh, but nourishes and cherishes it, just as Christ also does the church, because we are members of His body. For this reason a man shall leave his father and mother and shall be joined to his wife, and the two shall become one flesh. This mystery is great; but I am speaking with reference to Christ and the church. Nevertheless, each individual among you also is to love his own wife even as himself, and the wife must see to it that she respects her husband.

Colossians 3:19—Husbands, love your wives and do not be embittered against them.

1 Peter 3:7—You husbands in the same way, live with your wives in an understanding way, as with someone weaker, since she is a woman; and show her honor as a fellow heir of the grace of life, so that your prayers will not be hindered.

II.
REAL MEN SHEPHERD THEIR FAMILIES (EPHESIANS 5–6)

Deuteronomy 6:5-7—You shall love the LORD your God with all your heart and with all your soul and with all your might. These words, which I am commanding you today, shall be on your heart. You shall teach them diligently to your sons and shall talk of them when you sit in your house and when you walk by the way and when you lie down and when you rise up.

Psalm 78:4-7—We will not conceal them from their children, but tell to the generation to come the praises of the LORD, and His strength and His wondrous works that He has done. For He established a testimony in Jacob and appointed a law in Israel, which He commanded our fathers that they should teach them to their children, that the generation to come might know, even the children yet to be born, that they may arise and tell them to their children, that they should put their confidence in God and not forget the works of God, but keep His commandments.

Proverbs 13:24—He who withholds his rod hates his son, but he who loves him disciplines him diligently.

Proverbs 22:6,15—Train up a child in the way he should go, even when he is old he will not depart from it...Foolishness is bound up in the heart of a child; the rod of discipline will remove it far from him.

Proverbs 29:15,17—The rod and reproof give wisdom, but a child who gets his own way brings shame to his mother...Correct your son, and he will give you comfort; he will also delight your soul.

Ephesians 6:1-4—Children, obey your parents in the Lord, for this is right. Honor your father and mother (which is the first commandment with a promise), so that it may be well with you, and that you may live long on the earth. Fathers, do not provoke your children to anger, but bring them up in the discipline and instruction of the Lord.

Colossians 3:20-21—Children, be obedient to your parents in all things, for this is well-pleasing to the Lord. Fathers, do not exasperate your children, so that they will not lose heart.

1 Timothy 3:4-5—[An elder] must be one who manages his own household well, keeping his children under control with all dignity (but if a man does not know how to manage his own household, how will he take care of the church of God?).

Hebrews 12:6-11—Those whom the Lord loves He disciplines, and He scourges every son whom He receives. It is for discipline that you endure; God deals with you as with sons; for what son is there whom his father does not discipline? But if you are without discipline, of which all have become partakers, then you are illegitimate children and not sons. Furthermore, we had earthly fathers to discipline us, and we respected them; shall we not much rather be subject to the Father of spirits, and live? For they disciplined us for a short time as seemed best to them, but He disciplines us for our good, so that we may share His holiness. All discipline for the moment seems not to be joyful, but sorrowful; yet to those who have been trained by it, afterwards it yields the peaceful fruit of righteousness.

12.

REAL MEN WORK HARD
(PROVERBS)

Genesis 2:7-8,15—Then the Lord God formed man of dust from the ground, and breathed into his nostrils the breath of life; and man became a living being. The LORD God planted a garden toward the east, in Eden; and there He placed the man whom He had formed…Then the LORD God took the man and put him into the garden of Eden to cultivate it and keep it.

Proverbs 6:6-11—Go to the ant, O sluggard, observe her ways and be wise, which, having no chief, officer or ruler, prepares her food in the summer and gathers her provision in the harvest. How long will you lie down, O sluggard? When will you arise from your sleep? "A little sleep, a little slumber, a little folding of the hands to rest"—your poverty will come in like a vagabond and your need like an armed man.

Proverbs 10:4-5—Poor is he who works with a negligent hand, but the hand of the diligent makes rich. He who gathers in summer is a son who acts wisely, but he who sleeps in harvest is a son who acts shamefully.

Proverbs 24:30-34—I passed by the field of the sluggard and by the vineyard of the man lacking sense, and behold, it was completely overgrown with thistles; its surface was covered with nettles, and its stone wall was broken down. When I saw, I reflected upon it; I looked, and received instruction. "A little sleep, a little slumber, a little folding of the hands to rest," then your poverty will come as a robber and your want like an armed man.

Proverbs 26:13-16—The sluggard says, "There is a lion in the road! A lion is in the open square!" As the door turns on its hinges, so does the sluggard on his bed. The sluggard buries his hand in the dish; he is weary of bringing it to his mouth again. The sluggard is wiser in his own eyes than seven men who can give a discreet answer.

Colossians 3:23-24—Whatever you do, do your work heartily, as for the Lord rather than for men, knowing that from the Lord you will receive the reward of the inheritance. It is the Lord Christ whom you serve.

2 Thessalonians 3:6-12—Now we command you, brethren, in the name of our Lord Jesus Christ, that you keep away from every brother who leads an unruly life and not according to the tradition which you received from us. For you yourselves know how you ought to follow our example, because we did not act in an undisciplined manner among you, nor did we eat anyone's bread without paying for it, but with labor and hardship we kept working night and day so that we would not be a burden to any of you; not because we do not have the right to this, but in order to offer ourselves as a model for you, so that you would follow our example. For even when we were with you, we used to give you this order: if anyone is not willing to work, then he is not to eat, either. For we hear that some among you are leading an undisciplined life, doing no work at all, but acting like busybodies. Now such persons we command and exhort in the Lord Jesus Christ to work in quiet fashion and eat their own bread.

1 Timothy 5:8—If anyone does not provide for his own, and especially for those of his household, he has denied the faith and is worse than an unbeliever.

13.

REAL MEN LOVE THEIR ENEMIES
(ELISHA)

Matthew 5:38-47—You have heard that it was said, "An eye for an eye, and a tooth for a tooth." But I say to you, do not resist an evil person; but whoever slaps you on your right cheek, turn the other to him also. If anyone wants to sue you and take your shirt, let him have your coat also. Whoever forces you to go one mile, go with him two. Give to him who asks of you, and do not turn away from him who wants to borrow from you. You have heard that it was said, "You shall love your neighbor and hate your enemy." But I say to you, love your enemies and pray for those who persecute you, so that you may be sons of your Father who is in heaven; for He causes His sun to rise on the evil and the good, and sends rain on the righteous and the unrighteous. For if you love those who love you, what reward do you have? Do not even the tax collectors do the same? If you greet only your brothers, what more are you doing than others? Do not even the Gentiles do the same?

Romans 12:17-20—Never pay back evil for evil to anyone. Respect what is right in the sight of all men. If possible, so far as it depends on you, be at peace with all men. Never take your own revenge, beloved, but leave room for the wrath of God, for it is written, "Vengeance is Mine, I will repay," says the Lord. "But if your enemy is hungry, feed him, and if he is thirsty, give him a drink; for in so doing you will heap burning coals on his head."

1 Peter 2:20-24—What credit is there if, when you sin and are harshly treated, you endure it with patience? But if when you do what is right and suffer for it you patiently endure it, this finds favor with God. For you have been called for this purpose, since Christ also suffered for you, leaving you an example for you to follow in His steps, who committed no sin, nor was any deceit found in His mouth; and while being reviled, He did not revile in return; while suffering, He uttered no threats, but kept entrusting Himself to Him who judges righteously; and He Himself bore our sins in His body on the cross, so that we might die to sin and live to righteousness; for by His wounds you were healed.

1 Peter 3:14-17—Even if you should suffer for the sake of righteousness, you are blessed. And do not fear their intimidation, and do not be troubled, but sanctify Christ as Lord in your hearts, always being ready to make a defense to everyone who asks you to give an account for the hope that is in you, yet with gentleness and reverence; and keep a good conscience so that in the thing in which you are slandered, those who revile your good behavior in Christ will be put to shame.

1 John 4:7-11—Beloved, let us love one another, for love is from God; and everyone who loves is born of God and knows God. The one who does not love does not know God, for God is love. By this the love of God was manifested in us, that God has sent His only begotten Son into the world so that we might live through Him. In this is love, not that we loved God, but that He loved us and sent His Son to be the propitiation for our sins. Beloved, if God so loved us, we also ought to love one another.

14.
REAL MEN SHARE THE GOSPEL
(ACTS)

Matthew 5:14-16—You are the light of the world. A city set on a hill cannot be hidden; nor does anyone light a lamp and put it under a basket, but on the lampstand, and it gives light to all who are in the house. Let your light shine before men in such a way that they may see your good works, and glorify your Father who is in heaven.

Matthew 28:18-20—Jesus came up and spoke to them, saying, "All authority has been given to Me in heaven and on earth. Go therefore and make disciples of all the nations, baptizing them in the name of the Father and the Son and the Holy Spirit, teaching them to observe all that I commanded you; and lo, I am with you always, even to the end of the age."

Luke 24:45-47—He [Jesus] opened their minds to understand the Scriptures, and He said to them, "Thus it is written, that the Christ would suffer and rise again from the dead the third day, and that repentance for forgiveness of sins would be proclaimed in His name to all the nations, beginning from Jerusalem."

Romans 1:16—I am not ashamed of the gospel, for it is the power of God for salvation to everyone who believes, to the Jew first and also to the Greek.

Romans 10:9-15—If you confess with your mouth Jesus as Lord, and believe in your heart that God raised Him from the dead, you will be saved; for with the heart a person believes, resulting in righteousness, and with the mouth he confesses, resulting in salvation. For the Scripture says, "Whoever believes in Him will not be disappointed." For there is no distinction between Jew and Greek; for the same Lord is

Lord of all, abounding in riches for all who call on Him; for "Whoever will call on the name of the Lord will be saved." How then will they call on Him in whom they have not believed? How will they believe in Him whom they have not heard? And how will they hear without a preacher? How will they preach unless they are sent? Just as it is written, "How beautiful are the feet of those who bring good news of good things!"

Ephesians 6:19-20—Pray on my behalf, that utterance may be given to me in the opening of my mouth, to make known with boldness the mystery of the gospel, for which I am an ambassador in chains; that in proclaiming it I may speak boldly, as I ought to speak.

2 Timothy 4:1-2,5—I solemnly charge you in the presence of God and of Christ Jesus, who is to judge the living and the dead, and by His appearing and His kingdom: preach the word; be ready in season and out of season; reprove, rebuke, exhort, with great patience and instruction…Be sober in all things, endure hardship, do the work of an evangelist, fulfill your ministry.

1 Peter 2:12—Keep your behavior excellent among the Gentiles, so that in the thing in which they slander you as evildoers, they may because of your good deeds, as they observe them, glorify God in the day of visitation.

15.
REAL MEN LOVE THE CHURCH
(PAUL)

Matthew 16:18—I will build My church; and the gates of Hades will not overpower it.

1 Corinthians 12:13-27—By one Spirit we were all baptized into one body, whether Jews or Greeks, whether slaves or free, and we were all made to drink of one Spirit.

For the body is not one member, but many. If the foot says, "Because I am not a hand, I am not a part of the body," it is not for this reason any the less a part of the body. And if the ear says, "Because I am not an eye, I am not a part of the body," it is not for this reason any the less a part of the body. If the whole body were an eye, where would the hearing be? If the whole were hearing, where would the sense of smell be? But now God has placed the members, each one of them, in the body, just as He desired. If they were all one member, where would the body be? But now there are many members, but one body. And the eye cannot say to the hand, "I have no need of you"; or again the head to the feet, "I have no need of you." On the contrary, it is much truer that the members of the body which seem to be weaker are necessary; and those members of the body which we deem less honorable, on these we bestow more abundant honor, and our less presentable members become much more presentable, whereas our more presentable members have no need of it. But God has so composed the body, giving more abundant honor to that member which lacked, so that there may be no division in the body, but that the members may have the same care for one another. And if one member suffers, all the members suffer with it; if one member is honored, all the members rejoice with it.

Now you are Christ's body, and individually members of it.

2 Corinthians 11:26-28—I [Paul] have been on frequent journeys, in dangers from rivers, dangers from robbers, dangers from my countrymen, dangers from the Gentiles, dangers in the city, dangers in the wilderness, dangers on the sea, dangers among false brethren; I have been in labor and hardship, through many sleepless nights, in hunger and thirst, often without food, in cold and exposure. Apart from such external things, there is the daily pressure on me of concern for all the churches.

Ephesians 2:19-22—You are no longer strangers and aliens, but you are fellow citizens with the saints, and are of God's household, having been built on the foundation of the apostles and prophets, Christ Jesus Himself being the corner stone, in whom the whole building, being fitted together, is growing into a holy temple in the Lord, in whom you also are being built together into a dwelling of God in the Spirit.

Ephesians 5:25-27—Christ also loved the church and gave Himself up for her, so that He might sanctify her, having cleansed her by the washing of water with the word, that He might present to Himself the church in all her glory, having no spot or wrinkle or any such thing; but that she would be holy and blameless.

1 Timothy 3:15— I write so that you will know how one ought to conduct himself in the household of God, which is the church of the living God, the pillar and support of the truth.

Hebrews 10:23-25—Let us hold fast the confession of our hope without wavering, for He who promised is faithful; and let us consider how to stimulate one another to love and good deeds, not forsaking our own assembling together, as is the habit of some, but encouraging one another; and all the more as you see the day drawing near.

1 Peter 4:10-11—As each one has received a special gift, employ it in serving one another as good stewards of the manifold grace of God. Whoever speaks, is to do so as one who is speaking the utterances of God; whoever serves is to do so as one who is serving by the strength which God supplies; so that in all things God may be glorified through Jesus Christ, to whom belongs the glory and dominion forever and ever. Amen.

APPENDIX:
REAL MEN PURSUE PURITY

Job 31:1—I have made a covenant with my eyes; how then could I gaze at a virgin?

Psalm 119:9-11—How can a young man keep his way pure? By keeping it according to Your word. With all my heart I have sought You; do not let me wander from Your commandments. Your word I have treasured in my heart, that I may not sin against You.

Proverbs 5:20-23—Why should you, my son, be exhilarated with an adulteress and embrace the bosom of a foreigner? For the ways of a man are before the eyes of the LORD, and He watches all his paths. [The sinner's] own iniquities will capture the wicked, and he will be held with the cords of his sin. He will die for lack of instruction, and in the greatness of his folly he will go astray.

Matthew 5:27-30—You have heard that it was said, "You shall not commit adultery"; but I say to you that everyone who looks at a woman with lust for her has already committed adultery with her in his heart. If your right eye makes you stumble, tear it out and throw it from you; for it is better for you to lose one of the parts of your body, than for your whole body to be thrown into hell. If your right hand makes you stumble, cut it off and throw it from you; for it is better for you to lose one of the parts of your body, than for your whole body to go into hell.

Romans 13:12-14—The night is almost gone, and the day is near. Therefore let us lay aside the deeds of darkness and put on the armor of light. Let us behave properly as in the day, not in carousing and drunkenness, not in sexual promiscuity and sensuality, not in strife and jealousy. But put on the Lord Jesus Christ, and make no provision for the flesh in regard to its lusts.

1 Corinthians 6:9-11—Do you not know that the unrighteous will not inherit the kingdom of God? Do not be deceived; neither fornicators, nor idolaters, nor adulterers, nor effeminate, nor homosexuals, nor thieves, nor the covetous, nor drunkards, nor revilers, nor swindlers, will inherit the kingdom of God. Such were some of you; but you were washed, but you were sanctified, but you were justified in the name of the Lord Jesus Christ and in the Spirit of our God.

2 Corinthians 12:21—I am afraid that when I come again…I may mourn over many of those who have sinned in the past and not repented of the impurity, immorality and sensuality which they have practiced.

Ephesians 5:3-5—Immorality or any impurity or greed must not even be named among you, as is proper among saints; and there must be no filthiness and silly talk, or coarse jesting, which are not fitting, but rather giving of thanks. For this you know with certainty, that no immoral or impure person or covetous man, who is an idolater, has an inheritance in the kingdom of Christ and God.

Colossians 3:5-7—Consider the members of your earthly body as dead to immorality, impurity, passion, evil desire, and greed, which amounts to idolatry. For it is because of these things that the wrath of God will come upon the sons of disobedience, and in them you also once walked, when you were living in them.

1 Thessalonians 4:3-7—This is the will of God, your sanctification; that is, that you abstain from sexual immorality; that each of you know how to possess his own vessel in sanctification and honor, not in lustful passion, like the Gentiles who do not know God; and that no man transgress and defraud his brother in the matter because the Lord is the avenger in all these things, just as we also told you before and solemnly warned you. For God has not called us for the purpose of impurity, but in sanctification.

Hebrews 13:4—Marriage is to be held in honor among all, and the marriage bed is to be undefiled; for fornicators and adulterers God will judge.

Notes

CHAPTER 1—REAL MEN LIVE BY FAITH (ABRAHAM)

1. Eugene H. Merrill, *Kingdom of Priests* (Grand Rapids: Baker, 1996), 26.
2. Flavius Josephus, *Antiquities of the Jews*, 1:7.

CHAPTER 4—REAL MEN PRAY WITH BOLDNESS (ELIJAH)

1. J.C. Ryle, *A Call to Prayer: An Urgent Plea to Enter into the Secret Place* (Laurel, MS: Audubon Press, n.d.), 35.
2. William Varner, *The Chariot of Israel: Exploits of the Prophet Elijah,* 4th ed. (Bellmawr, NJ: The Friends of Israel Gospel Ministry, 1991), 22.

CHAPTER 5—REAL MEN LOVE TO WORSHIP (HYMN WRITERS OF ISRAEL)

1. Jonathan Edwards, "Ethical Writings" in *The Works of Jonathan Edwards Series*, Vol. 8, gen. ed. Paul Ramsey (New Haven, CT: Yale University Press, 1989), 442.
2. John Piper, *God's Passion for His Glory* (Wheaton, IL: Crossway, 1998), 83.
3. Martin Luther, *A Manual of the Book of Psalms,* trans. Henry Cole (London: Seeley and Burnside, 1837), 220.
4. C.H. Spurgeon, *The Treasury of David* (Peabody, MA: Hendrickson Publishers, n.d.), 1:324.
5. Charles Wesley, "And Can It Be That I Should Gain."

CHAPTER 6—REAL MEN FLEE TEMPTATION (TIMOTHY)

1. John Owen, "Of the Mortification of Sin in Believers," in *Overcoming Sin and Temptation,* eds. Kelly Kapic and Justin Taylor (Wheaton, IL: Crossway, 2006), 50.
2. Matthew Henry, *The Matthew Henry Commentary,* ed. Leslie F. Church, PhD (Grand Rapids: Zondervan, 1961), 1896.

CHAPTER 7—REAL MEN REPENT FROM SIN (DAVID)

1. C.H. Spurgeon, "Gray Hairs," a sermon delivered on September 13, 1868, in *The Metropolitan Tabernacle Pulpit* (Pasadena, TX: Pilgrim Publications, 1969), 14:509.
2. Robert D. Bergen, "1 & 2 Samuel," in *The New American Commentary,* ed. E. Ray Clendenen (Nashville: Broadman & Holman, 1996), 364. Cf. 2 Samuel 16:23; 23:34,39.
3. Thomas Watson, as cited in *The Golden Treasury of Puritan Quotations*, compiled by I.D.E. Thomas (Edinburgh: Banner of Truth, 1975), 240.

4. Andrew Murray, *Have Mercy Upon Me: The Prayer of the Penitent in the Fifty-first Psalm Explained and Applied,* trans. J.P. Lilley (London: James Nisbet, 1896), 58.

5. C.H. Spurgeon, *The Treasury of David* (Peabody, MA: Hendrickson Publishers, n.d.), 1:403.

6. Perowne, J.J. Stewart, *The Book of Psalms: A New Translation with Introduction and Notes* (George Bell and Sons, 1878; reprint, Grand Rapids: Zondervan, 1976), 421.

CHAPTER 8—REAL MEN REFUSE TO COMPROMISE (DANIEL)

1. John MacArthur, *The Power of Integrity* (Wheaton, IL: Crossway, 1997), 67.

2. Ibid.

CHAPTER 9—REAL MEN LEAD WITH COURAGE (NEHEMIAH)

1. C.T. Studd, *The Chocolate Soldier, or, Heroism—The Lost Chord of Christianity* (Fort Washington, PA: Christian Literature Crusade, n.d.). Online book available at http://www.gutenberg.org/ebooks/22331.

2. Ibid.

CHAPTER 10—REAL MEN LOVE THEIR WIVES (PETER)

1. John MacArthur, *Ephesians* (Chicago: Moody, 1986), 300.

2. D. Edmond Hiebert, *1 Peter* (Winona Lake, IN: BMH Books, 1992), 207.

3. John MacArthur, *1 Peter* (Chicago: Moody, 2004), 182-83.

4. Clement of Alexandria, *Miscellanies Book VII,* eds. Fenton John Anthoy Hort and Joseph B. Mayor (London: MacMillan, 1902), 140.

5. Cf. *Eusebius: The Church History,* trans. Paul L. Maier (Grand Rapids: Kregel, 1999), 93.

CHAPTER 11—REAL MEN SHEPHERD THEIR FAMILIES (EPHESIANS 5–6)

1. Author unknown. Cited from John MacArthur, *Ephesians* (Chicago: Moody, 1986), 318-19.

CHAPTER 12—REAL MEN WORK HARD (PROVERBS)

1. Charles Bridges, *Proverbs* (London: Banner of Truth, 1979), 61.

2. Associated Press, "Survey: More Americans Unhappy At Work," January 5, 2010, http://www.cbsnews.com/stories/2010/01/05/national/main6056611.shtml.

3. Alexander Maclaren, as cited in W.R. Moody, ed., *Record of Christian Work,* vol. 24 (East Northfield, MA: W.R. Moody, 1910), 338.

CHAPTER 15—REAL MEN LOVE THE CHURCH (PAUL)

1. Charles Spurgeon, "The Best Donation" (No. 2234), an exposition of 2 Corinthians 8:5 delivered on April 5, 1891 at the Metropolitan Tabernacle in London, England.

2. Ibid.

APPENDIX 1—REAL MEN PURSUE PURITY

1. John MacArthur, *1 & 2 Thessalonians* (Chicago: Moody, 2002), 109.

2. John MacArthur, *Romans 1–8* (Chicago: Moody, 1991), 85-86.

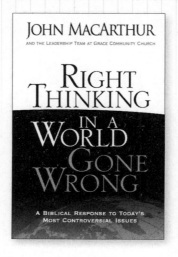
One of the greatest challenges facing Christians today is the powerful influence of secular thinking. From all directions we're fed a constant barrage of persuasive—yet unbiblical—worldviews. This makes it difficult to know where to stand on today's most talked-about issues.

The leadership team at Grace Community Church, along with their pastor, John MacArthur, provide much-needed discernment and clarity in the midst of rampant confusion. Using the Bible as the foundation, you'll learn how to develop a Christian perspective on key issues—including...

political activism	environmentalism
the cult of celebrity	entertainment and escapism
homosexual marriage	abortion, birth control, & surrogacy
euthanasia and suicide	disasters and epidemics
immigration	God and the problem of evil

Also included is a topical reference guide to Bible verses that address key concerns—a guide that will arm you with right thinking and biblical answers to challenging questions.